Sailors of the Concrete Sea

❖

The Sloan Foundation Trucking Industry Program (TIP) driver survey conducted 573 interviews with truck drivers at nineteen truck stops in the Midwest between July and October in 1997. The data collected from this effort provides a comprehensive portrait of the driving workforce, of the work of truck drivers, and of their opinions about their jobs. Analysis of the data addresses issues of immediate policy interest, including how drivers respond to public regulation of their work; how frequently drivers have problems with drowsiness, illness, and injuries; and their views of government policies. It also provides detailed information, lacking in other studies, about hours drivers spend driving as well as time spent on nondriving duties; on drivers' use and views of new technologies; on compensation systems, including benefits such as pensions, health insurance, vacation, and holiday time; and on supplemental retirement systems.

Sailors of the Concrete Sea provides an overview of the information collected by this survey in more than seventy charts and forty tables plus supporting text. It was written in cooperation with The Survey Research Center of the Institute of Social Research, University of Michigan, and funded by the Alfred P. Sloan Foundation.

❖

Sailors
of the
Concrete Sea

A Portrait of Truck Drivers' Work and Lives

From the 1997 Survey of Truck Drivers
Sloan Foundation Trucking Industry Program

Dale L. Belman
Kristen A. Monaco
Taggert J. Brooks

Michigan State University Press • *East Lansing, Michigan*

∞ The paper used in this publication meets the minimum requirements
of ANSI/NISO Z39.48-1992 (R 1997) (Permanence of Paper).

Michigan State University Press
East Lansing, Michigan 48823-5245

Printed and bound in the United States of America.

11 10 09 08 07 06 05   1 2 3 4 5 6 7 8 9 10

LIBRARY OF CONGRESS CATALOGING-IN-PUBLICATION DATA
Sailors of the concrete sea : a portrait of truck drivers' work and lives /
Dale L. Belman, Kristen A. Monaco, Taggert J. Brooks.
p. cm.
Includes bibliographical references.
ISBN 0-87013-686-0 (pbk. : alk. paper)
1. Truck drivers—United States 2. Social surveys—United States
3. Truck driving—United States I. Title.
HD8039.M7952 U524 2004 2005
388.3/24/0973—dc22
2004053897

Cover and book design by Sharp Des!gns, Inc.
Cover photo by Kristen A. Monaco.

Visit Michigan State University Press on the World Wide Web at *www.msupress.msu.edu*

Contents

Figures

Tables

Acknowledgments

Successful completion of a research survey of this magnitude requires the efforts of many people as the work proceeds.

The most important participants were the drivers themselves. Drivers work long hours under difficult conditions. They were asked to answer detailed and controversial questions. Oftentimes they were answering the survey after ten or more hours of work, in locations that were far from comfortable. We were most fortunate that the drivers were so willing to participate and that even those who decided not to participate were unfailingly courteous and helpful. We hope that they find this research both interesting and useful.

We are also grateful to the graduate students and interviewers from the Institute for Social Research (ISR) at the University of Michigan and the University of Wisconsin Milwaukee who collected this data. Interviewing is a talent that requires an ability to establish rapport with the subject combined with precision in conveying questions and noting answers. This survey demanded a great deal from the interviewers, keeping them in truck stops in the Midwest for much of the months of July, August, September, and October 1997. Their dedication and care were critical to the success of this study.

Thanks are also due to a number of individuals who played important roles in the study. First, thanks are due to Beth Pennington and Fleurette Saari, employees of the ISR. Beth and Fleurette provided leadership for the eastern and western interview teams, furthered the training of graduate students, and helped arrange the staffing of the teams. Beth also performed an essential role in piloting the survey, assessing drivers' reactions, and consequently revising the survey.

Lisa Holland and Julie Ballin of the ISR likewise deserve high praise for their work. Julie oversaw the production and distribution of the questionnaires, the arrangement and coordination of the interview teams, and the processing of the completed interviews. The quality and care of her work, her willingness to put time and effort into the project, and her good humor in the face of adversities helped the survey run smoothly. The project would not have come to pass without the efforts of Lisa Holland, the manager of the survey for the ISR. She worked with academics who lacked background in survey research and over the course of a year provided the guidance and the oversight needed to produce a high-quality survey. We could not have hoped for a better teacher.

We also acknowledge and give thanks for the extensive support provided by the Institute for Social Research sampling staff, particularly Steven Heeringa and Judy Connor. Our confidence in the representativeness of our survey rests on their expertise and their ability to elucidate difficult but essential knowledge about sampling.

On the Sloan Foundation Trucking Industry Program (TIP) side of this research, we are grateful to Dr. Peter Swan for his work coordinating the TIP members on the eastern survey team. We are particularly grateful to Dr. Michael Belzer, associate director of TIP for human resource research, for his aid in the initial stages of the survey, his work on the questionnaire, and his help with the revision of the chartbook. Mike's knowledge of trucking has helped to guide our research throughout. Thanks also to Professors Chelsea White III and Robert Haessler, co-directors of TIP, for their unfailing support.

Acknowledgment and gratitude is also owed to the Alfred P. Sloan foundation, which has provided the generous funding for TIP and this project. It is rare for researchers to be afforded the opportunity to engage in this type of primary research, and we are grateful for this unique opportunity. We also owe a debt of gratitude to our project officers, Dr. Hirsh Cohen and Dr. Gail Pesyna, who have supported and guided TIP and the driver survey since their inception.

Some special acknowledgments are owed to the graduate students who were central to the success of this survey. First, to Stephen Burks, currently Assistant Professor of Economics at the University of Minnesota Morris, who initially suggested a driver survey and who was deeply involved in the development of the questionnaire and the sampling structure. His background in truck driving helped focus the questionnaire on essential issues. Second, to T. J. Brooks, currently Assistant Professor of Economics at the University of Wisconsin La Crosse, whose involvement began with his work on a survey team and has continued into data analysis and the writing of this report. Both of these students have given freely of their time and made critical contributions. Finally, particular thanks are due to Dr. Kristen Monaco, now Professor of Economics at California State University, Long Beach. Kristen was involved in all stages of this survey, led the western survey team, provided essential financial support to her team on occasion with her unstinting use of her credit card, and delayed completing her dissertation because of her work on the survey. I could not have hoped for a better graduate assistant, and I have been fortunate in continued association as her colleague.

Finally, I wish to thank my wife, Amy Wells, who, with unfailing good humor, encouraged this research and endured the time and absences it entailed.

DALE BELMAN
Director, TIP Driver Survey

Introduction

Sailors of the Concrete Sea provides a cross-section of the data collected by the 1997 Sloan Foundation Survey of Truck Drivers, presented in the form of charts and tables with supporting text. The data presented in this report is taken from the 573 long surveys collected in July, August, September, and October of that year. It addresses topics such as driver mileage and earnings, educational attainment, driver tenure, work time, and the use of technology on trucks. It is intended as a descriptive rather than an analytic report, although some analysis is provided in the text. Future TIP reports will provide analytic approaches to issues such as the effect of technology on driver efficiency and earnings. Appendices to this report include the text of the surveys and a description of the sampling procedures.

The report provides new data on issues currently facing the freight industry. The survey documents problems surrounding drivers' working hours. We find that the majority of drivers work up to or beyond the sixty hours permitted by the Hours of Service Regulations. The survey also suggests that long hours are a result both of pressures from freight firms and shippers and of drivers' efforts to maintain middle-class incomes. We provide some new insight on the driver shortage. We find that although drivers have a strong commitment to their occupation, they spend little time with any one firm. The typical respondent had worked as a driver for twelve years, but had worked for his or her current employer for only eighteen months. One-quarter of respondents had quit a job in the last year. This suggests that what appears to firms to be the consequences of a driver shortage is significantly the result of very high levels of turnover of drivers who remain in the industry. Efforts aimed at improving driver retention might be the most effective means for firms to reduce their recruitment costs and reduce the apparent effect of the shortage.

Contrary to the usual view of drivers as perennial loners, the family life of drivers was found to be similar to that of other blue-collar workers. In fact, drivers are more likely to be married and less likely to be divorced then other blue-collar workers. They are also more likely to have children, and to have more children than other blue-collar workers. More in keeping with their public image, however, we do find that drivers favor country music programming when working.

This book had two purposes: to document the work and work life of truck drivers and to show the wealth of material available in the driver survey. The survey has enabled us to investigate some of common beliefs about drivers. Prior to this survey, there was little accurate information about driver's hours of work. Although long hours of work were acknowledged, violations of hours of service regulations were often ascribed to a few "bad actors." Our research has documented that working beyond the sixty hour rule is ubiquitous as are other violations of hours of service regulations. It is no longer reasonable to argue that the typical driver is following the legal limitations on driving. Similarly, there has been a long running debate over whether owner-operators are better off than employee drivers. Our data provides a nuanced answer to this debate. We find that although the earnings of the typical owner-operator are similar to those of employee drivers, about one quarter of owner-operators are earning substantially more and a similar percentage seem to be earning substantially less than employee drivers. Data from the driver survey have also allowed us to examine topics such as driver turnover, the structure of compensation and benefits, drivers views of their work and their use of technology in far greater detail than has been possible in the past. This detail allows both a broader and more in depth understanding of truck driving.

The material that has been included in this book represents only a modest amount of the data collected in the first wave of the survey. There are more than six hundred variables in the TIP driver survey data set, and relatively little of this has been presented in this book or other published research. There is considerable additional detail on issues such as pay and benefits, the characteristics of owner-operators and their business, health and safety, and employees' views of their work, their employers, and of unions that remains to be explored. To facilitate the use of this data, we have included the first wave data set on the CD that accompanies this book. The data set is provided in STATA, SAS, and SPSS format and can be readily converted to formats for other statistical programs using STATRANS or equivalent programs. We do request that any work that uses this data cite it as the "Sloan Foundation Trucking Industry Program Driver Survey" and indicate that it was collected by the Trucking Industry Program at the Georgia Institute of Technology.

Overview of the Driver Survey

The motor freight industry has evolved rapidly over the twenty years since deregulation. Technology, firm structure, the requirements of shippers, and the array of services provided by the industry are all, as other parts of this report indicate, undergoing substantial and persistent change. What has not changed in this industry is that movement of goods still depends on a person driving a load from its point of origin to its destination and doing that job dependably. Despite the evolution of the industry, payroll continued to account for 27.7% of industry revenue in 1992. Labor is central to the operation of the industry.

The industry, the public, employee associations, scholars, and the drivers themselves are confronted by industry labor force issues. The industry has, for many years, been unable to recruit adequate numbers of appropriately trained employees, or to retain employees who have been trained. The public has confronted issues involving the safety of the motor freight transportation system with particular concerns about driver fatigue brought on by hours of work in violation of the Hours of Service Regulations. The evolution of the industry has pushed employee representatives, particularly the International Brotherhood of Teamsters, into steadily less important roles. Their ability to represent members and organize additional members depends, in part, on their ability to reestablish their reputation among drivers. Scholars have interests in numerous issues, particularly those that revolve around the relationship between the quality of jobs and work and the output of those jobs: productivity, dependability, driver health, and public safety. Finally, the drivers themselves have suffered from declining wages, increasing hours, and deterioration in other working conditions for more than twenty years.

Despite the importance of employee issues, relatively little is known about the nature of work, the characteristics of employees, or the structure of the employment relationship in the industry. With the exception of Belzer (1993), research has been limited to analysis of secondary data sets that have not been specific to trucking and that have not collected much of the information required to address industry issues. This survey has been designed to provide preliminary answers to questions on the more pressing current issues, as well as to other, less immediate questions. Extensive queries on compensation, driving and nondriving hours of work, job duties, work history, and industry segment allow us to document worker characteristics, conditions of work, and the views of drivers in the various segments of the industry. This provides the foundation needed to discuss the issues confronting the industry.

Data Collection

The survey instrument was developed and administered in cooperation with the Survey Research Center (SRC) of the Institute for Social Research (ISR) of the University of Michigan. The ISR, which recently entered its fiftieth year, is a preeminent social science research institute with a considerable history in survey research, including administration of the Panel Study of Income Dynamics. The instruments used for the driver survey took approximately six months to develop, including the three pilot surveys used to test the questionnaires.

The Instruments

Two survey instruments were used in this study: a long survey, which took approximately forty minutes to complete, and a short survey, which collected data for a limited subset of questions from the long survey and took approximately five minutes to complete.

The long survey (see appendix 2) collected data on eight topics: work history, industry segment, job and trip characteristics and compensation, demographics, technology, use of logbooks and attitudes toward Hours of Service Regulation, views about current employers and of unions, and views about future opportunities in the industry. The chapter on job and trip characteristics and compensation was structured so that employee drivers and owner-operators were asked somewhat different questions. In all, the long questionnaire collected data on more than 210 items.

The long surveys were administered in the truck stops, typically in the restaurant or café, but sometimes in the television room, in the truckers' lounge, in the video arcade, or on a convenient countertop.

The short questionnaire (see appendix 3) performed two functions. First, the researchers had concerns that the length of the long questionnaire would preclude drivers who were under time constraints from answering the questions. The shorter questionnaire was a means of soliciting information from drivers when they were unable or unwilling to participate in the long questionnaire. Most short questionnaires were, however, administered on fuel lines. The purpose of the fuel line surveys was to broaden the sample to represent all drivers entering the truck stop, not just those who stopped to have a meal or take an extended break. The fuel line surveys also allowed researchers to determine whether there were systematic differences between those who had time for the long survey and those who were just stopping for fuel or lacked time for the longer questionnaire.

Sampling Methodology

Randomness in sampling is essential to the construction of representative data. The end result of the sampling scheme is, ideally, that all drivers in the target population, drivers in the motor freight industry working in the Midwest, would have an equal chance of being chosen for the survey. This study utilized a two-stage randomized design to assure that it was reasonably representative.

The first stage involved the selection of truck stops at which the surveys would be conducted. There is little information on systematic differences between drivers who stop at different types of truck stops. Broad coverage of truck stops of different sizes and traffic density was therefore important to assure that all types of drivers were included in this study. Locations were stratified into groups by the number of parking spaces (size) and by state. The number of truck stops selected from each size or state group was determined by the proportion of parking accounted for by that group. Selection of locations within the size or state groups was randomized. A variety of truck stops were covered by the survey teams. The largest was a stop in Effingham, Illinois, the site of one of the largest groups of truck stops in North America. We also interviewed drivers in several small "lunch" truck stops in the rural counties of Wisconsin, Michigan, and Ohio. Some truck stops were relatively pleasant "family" stops, while others were notably rougher. Subsequent statistical analysis has indicated moderate differences in the characteristics of respondents between small and large truck stops.

Interviews at the truck stops were also randomized by day, time, and individual to provide a representative sample and prevent interviewer bias from affecting the selection of subjects. Interview teams remained at truck stops for two consecutive weekdays, with the start day chosen at random from among the five weekdays.[1] Interviews were conducted in three-hour shifts, which began at fixed hours between 6:00 A.M. and 10:00 P.M. Interviews were conducted during six to eight shifts over the two days, with shifts randomly assigned.

Intake of subjects was also randomized. All individuals who were not obviously ineligible, such as young children or individuals with disabilities that would legally preclude them from operating a commercial vehicle, were counted on entering the truck stop. Every n^{th} potentially eligible person entering was approached for screening, with the frequency of approach depending upon the density of traffic. As few as one in every ten and as many as every person entering the truck stop were approached and screened. Eligibility was contingent on the individual identifying him- or herself as a truck driver, as currently driving a truck, and as holding a commercial driver's license. If drivers met these criteria they were asked to participate in the study. If the subject agreed, the interviewer read them the confidentiality statement and then started the interview. If the subject declined, the interviewer offered the possibility of doing the interview over the phone at a convenient time. If this opportunity was also declined, drivers were asked to complete a short survey. Respondents to the long survey were paid $20.00 for their aid, whether they did the survey in person or by phone. SRC interviewers who had worked as interviewers at truck stops conducted telephone interviews of drivers. The in-person surveys were completed in October 1997; efforts to obtain phone interviews were ended on 31 December 1997.

Administration and Quality Control

The accuracy of survey results depends on accuracy in the administration of the survey by the interviewer and adherence to protocols.

Interview teams were composed of permanent SRC interviewers, graduate students associated with TIP, graduate students hired specifically for this research, and retired truck drivers. All interviewers working on this project received two days of training from the SRC in Ann Arbor, Michigan. The first day included familiarization with SRC interview procedures; a presentation on the industry and drivers by Christopher Varsos, Business Agent from IBT Local 200; a question-by-question presentation of the long survey; and a role-play of an interview. On the second day non-SRC interviewer trainees were paired with experienced SRC interviewers to practice approaching and interviewing drivers at a truck stop ten miles west of Ann Arbor. Once interviewers were in the field, SRC employees provided oversight for teams to assure that protocols were followed and that interviews were conducted according to SRC methods.

Success of the Data Collection Process

The accuracy of a survey depends, in part, on achieving reasonable response rates. Low rates of response may be indicative of response bias, nonrandom patterns in the type of subject who responds. Such response bias may result in a nonrepresentative sample. The typical means of increasing response rates is the use of "refusal conversions," returning to a subject and repeating the request that he or she participate. A stubborn subject may be asked to participate several times and eventually offered compensation to participate in the study. This was not possible in the driver survey, as the respondents were anonymous and there was no means of contacting refusals after they left the truck stop. Respondents were offered a twenty dollar incentive payment for participation in the long survey. Respondents who could or would not do a long survey at that time were offered the opportunity to do the survey over the phone at a more convenient time. If they remained unable or unwilling to do the phone survey, they were offered the opportunity to take the five-minute survey.

Despite the inability to do "refusal conversions," response rates on the driver survey were satisfactory. A total of 1,959 individuals were approached inside truck stops and screened for participation in the long survey. Of the 955 who were eligible for the survey, 414 completed the survey in person, 159 completed the survey over the phone, and 55 answered the five-minute survey. In all, more than two-thirds of the drivers who were approached participated in the survey. This is considerably better than the 50% response rates typically achieved in successful one-time interviewing. Our success reflects a well-designed survey and the capacity of the interviewers.

The fuel line surveys achieved higher response rates. Of the 221 trucks that stopped at the fuel line, it was possible to approach 194 drivers. Of these, 187 agreed to be interviewed and only 7 refused an interview.

The Chartbook

The data in the chartbook is presented to highlight important facts about the driver workforce and subgroups within that workforce. In most tables and charts, data is presented for the entire workforce and is then broken out by the employment relationship and the nature of the work. Two basic distinctions in the employment relationship are whether the respondent is an employee or owner-operator and whether he or she is a union member. The work of union drivers is regulated by a collective bargaining agreement, and their position is accordingly different than that of nonunion drivers. Owner-operators are self-employed and typically own their tractor if not their trailer. They assume considerable capital risk and often assume the burden of locating loads. Although much of the work done by owner-operators is similar to that of employees, there are sufficient differences to make separation of the data potentially fruitful. These distinctions would create a four-way division in the data, but only two owner-operators reported being union members. It is not possible to provide meaningful statistics on so small a sample, so we divide the data three ways: union employees, nonunion employees, and nonunion owner-operators.

The data is also divided by whether the respondent worked as an over-the-road (OTR) driver or as a local driver. This reflects differences in the nature of the work. Over-the-road drivers drive farther and make fewer stops to load or drop freight; local drivers drive fewer miles and spend more of their time on pickup and delivery work. Again, this distinction between types of work is a fruitful approach to characterizing drivers' work.

The Data CD

One of the charges of the Sloan Foundation was to encourage research on the trucking industry. The data used to create the chartbook is a uniquely rich and varied source of information on the trucking industry. The authors of this book and others have used a small part of the available data to explore some of the issues of the industry and of drivers. We have included data from the first wave of the survey on a CD that accompanies this book in the hope that it will be used to further explore and understand the work and work life of truck drivers. The data set is provided on the CD in STATA, SAS, and SPSS formats; documentation on the data is provided in the "Information on the Data CD.pdf" file on the CD.

CHAPTER 1

Who Was Interviewed

Who were the 573 drivers who took forty-five minutes for the long interview? The respondents could be described in many different ways, as the text and charts and tabulations of data in this report indicate. In this chapter we consider the drivers interviewed from three standpoints: the division of the industry in which they worked, where they lived, and their personal characteristics. The description of drivers' industry affiliation includes distinguishing whether they worked for a private carrier or a firm providing services for hire, the type of equipment they were driving when interviewed, and the commodity they were carrying.[1] Finally, personal information includes responses to questions about gender, race, ethnicity, marital status, number of children, and educational attainment.

Type of Driver and Use of Logbooks

For whom did our respondents work? What type of work did they do? What equipment did they use and what type of commodities were they hauling? All of these characteristics help define our respondents and assure that, overall, our sample was composed of fairly typical drivers. We begin with several distinctions between drivers, which we carry throughout this report. We typically first report data for the full pool of drivers, but then report separately for employees who are union members, employees who are not union members, and owner-operators who are not union members. We also provide data that distinguishes between over-the-road and local drivers. These divisions distinguish drivers who work under differing work structures and job requirements. They allow us to explore the degree to which these divisions translate into differences in the nature of the work and work life of the drivers.

Size and Composition of the Sample

Fifty of the 573 individuals who made up our sample were employees who belonged to a union, 369 were employees who did not belong to a union, 151 were owner-operators who did not belong to a union, 2 were owner-operators who belonged to a union.[2] In addition, 505 of the respondents described themselves as over-the-road drivers and 68 described themselves as local drivers.

These raw data are not directly representative of the population under study. Because of the design of the sample, it is necessary to weight the data with weights generated by the multistage sampling scheme.[3] Such weights are used through out this study unless otherwise noted. Once weighted, 11.1% of respondents were union employees,

■ Table 1. Types of Drivers

	ALL	OTR	LOCAL
All	100.0%	85.4%	14.6%
Union	11.5%	9.0%	2.6%
Nonunion	88.5%	76.4%	12.1%
Employee Drivers	74.5%	61.8%	12.7%
Union	11.1%	8.5%	2.6%
Nonunion	63.4%	53.3%	10.1%
Owner-Operators	25.5%	23.6%	2.0%
Union	0.5%	0.5%	0.0%
Nonunion	25.1%	23.1%	2.0%

63.4% were nonunion employees, 25.1% were nonunion owner-operators, and 0.5% were union owner-operators. Local drivers made up 14.6% of the sample; 85.4% were over-the-road drivers.

Logbooks

The Department of Transportation requires that motor freight drivers who drive more than one hundred miles from their domicile point on a regular basis keep a log of their on-duty time. Drivers for other industries, such as construction, and intra-urban local delivery drivers are not required to keep such logs. The proportion of the sample who keep logbooks is a measure of the proportion of respondents who are involved in interurban motor freight. Ninety-four percent of respondents reported that they kept a log. This did not vary significantly by employment relationship but it did vary by the nature of the work. Local drivers were the least likely to keep a log, with only slightly over two-thirds (68.1%) reporting that they used a log. Almost all drivers who described themselves as over-the-road drivers reported keeping a log. Additional discussion of issues involving logbooks can be found in the chapter on job pressures and regulation (chapter 7).

Unionization by Type of Driver

Union membership among truck drivers has fallen considerably over the twenty years since deregulation. Almost forty-three percent (42.5%) of the truck drivers included in the May 1978/1979 Current Population Survey (CPS), the national labor force survey used to determine the unemployment rate, indicated that they were union members. By 1997 this had declined to 19.6% of truck drivers.

Almost twelve percent (11.5%) of the respondents to the driver survey reported that they were currently union members. This is lower than the figure obtained from national samples, but the survey includes owner-operators, who are excluded from calculations of national membership and are less likely to be members than are employees. When the calculation is limited to employees, membership is 15.5%. The remaining difference is likely due to differences in the definition of truck driver between the CPS and the driver survey and the greater representation of local drivers in national surveys.

Owner-operators make up 25.5% of the interview sample, and few are union members. Nonunion owner-operators account for 25.1 percentage points, and union owner-operators account for 0.5 percentage points.[4] The number of union owner-operators in the sample is sufficiently small to make exact estimates of their role among owner-operators difficult. They certainly represent less than 5% of owner-operators, and may be a vanishingly small proportion of the owner-operator labor force.

Local drivers are substantially more likely to be union members than are over-the-road drivers. Union density, the proportion of union members in a population, is 10.5% among over-the-road drivers. In contrast, 17.6% of local drivers report they are union members. This is consistent with the pattern of union membership found in other studies.

Industry Affiliation, Equipment, and Load

Industry Affiliation

Turning initially to industry affiliation, we have followed the conventional breakdown of the motor freight industry into private carriage and for hire carriage. For the purposes of the survey drivers were asked to consider themselves private carriage drivers if the firm for which they worked was primarily engaged in a business other than motor freight. Respondents were asked to consider themselves as working for a for hire firm if their firm's primary business was moving freight. Those who responded that they worked for hire were asked whether they worked for a truck-load carrier (TL), a less-than-truck-load-carrier (LTL), or a firm that provided both services.[5] Data on industry affiliation is provided for all drivers, and is broken down between nonunion employees, union employees, and nonunion owner-operators. The two union owner-operators were excluded from the data on owner-operators, as they worked under different conditions than their nonorganized counterparts, but their numbers are included in the All Driver data.

■ Table 2. Industry Affiliations by Type of Employer

	ALL DRIVERS	EMPLOYEES		OWNER-OPERATORS
		UNION	NONUNION	(NONUNION)
Distribution between Private Carrier and For Hire by Type of Driver				
Private Carrier	17.0%	37.3%	15.5%	12.3%
For Hire	83.0%	62.7%	84.5%	87.7%
Distribution of Types of Drivers between Private Carrier and For Hire				
Private Carrier	24.2%	57.6%	18.2%	100%
For Hire	8.4%	64.6%	26.5%	100%
For Hire*		SUBSAMPLE OF FOR HIRE		
TL	72.5%	17.4%	87.2%	65.4%
LTL	17.6%	70.4%	7.1%	19.6%
Both	8.4%	12.5%	5.7%	11.1%
No Response	1.5%	0.0%	0.0%	4.0%

*Estimates are derived from a small sample and may have a large sample error.

Private carriage drivers accounted for 17% of all drivers in the survey, while 83% of drivers reported working for a for hire firm. Breaking this down by union and owner-operator status, union employees are more likely to work for nontrucking firms than are nonunion employees or owner-operators. One-third of union members worked in private carriage, and two-thirds worked in the for hire sector. In contrast, 15.5% of nonunion employees and 12.3% of nonunion owner-operators worked in private carriage, while 84.5% and 87.7%, respectively, worked in for hire. Despite the different distribution of union employees, nonunion employees, and owner-operators across private carriage and for hire firms, nonunion employees accounted for the majority of drivers in both sectors. In private carriage, 57.6% of drivers were nonunion employees, 24.2% were union employees, and 18.2% were nonunion

■ Figure 1. Types of Trailers

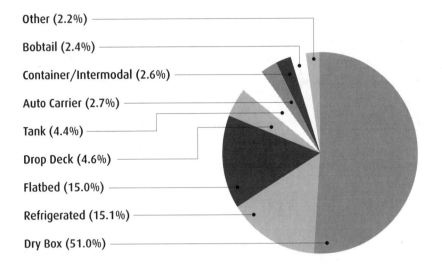

Other (2.2%)

Bobtail (2.4%)

Container/Intermodal (2.6%)

Auto Carrier (2.7%)

Tank (4.4%)

Drop Deck (4.6%)

Flatbed (15.0%)

Refrigerated (15.1%)

Dry Box (51.0%)

owner-operators. In for hire, 64.6% of drivers were nonunion employees, 26.5% were nonunion owner-operators, and only 8.4% were union employees.

Of the for hire drivers, a large majority, 72.5%, worked for TL firms, 17.6% worked for LTL firms, and 8.4% reported working for firms that provided both TL and LTL services. Again, distinguishing between union employees, nonunion employees, and owner-operators, union employees are mostly found in the LTL segment of the industry (70.4%). Most nonunion employees (87.2%) work for TL firms, and owner-operators are also largely in the TL segment of the For Hire segment (65.4%).

Equipment

Turning to type of equipment, more than half of the respondents (51.0%) reported driving nonrefrigerated (dry box) vans on their current trip. Refrigerated vans accounted for an additional 15.1% of the equipment. This is very close to the proportion of drivers with flatbed trucks (15.0%). More specialized equipment included drop deck (4.6%), tank (4.4%), auto carrier (2.7%), container or intermodal (2.6%), and other, including specialized heavy hauling (6.2%), trailers. Empty vans or tractors without trailers (bobtail) accounted for 2.4% of the sample.

Commodities

Although ninety-six distinct classifications of commodities were reported by the drivers, a relatively small number accounted for more than half of the sample (53.6%). Reflecting the importance of the automotive industry in the Midwest, trucks carrying motor vehicles and motor vehicle equipment made up 13.6% of the sample. Products of blast furnaces and steel mills, much of which also goes into automobiles, accounted for an additional 5.8% of shipments in the sample. Papermaking is also important in the upper Midwest, particularly in Wisconsin, and pulp, paper, and paperboard accounted for 4.5% of the sample. Groceries are a substantial proportion of the commodities in the sample: 4.2% of drivers reported carrying unspecified food products,

■ Figure 2. Fifteen Most Important Commodities Carried

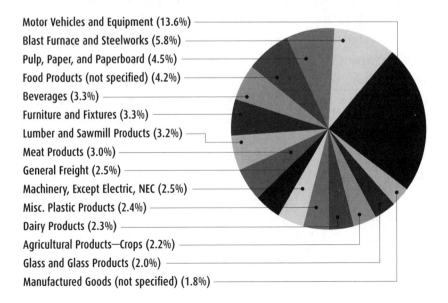

Motor Vehicles and Equipment (13.6%)
Blast Furnace and Steelworks (5.8%)
Pulp, Paper, and Paperboard (4.5%)
Food Products (not specified) (4.2%)
Beverages (3.3%)
Furniture and Fixtures (3.3%)
Lumber and Sawmill Products (3.2%)
Meat Products (3.0%)
General Freight (2.5%)
Machinery, Except Electric, NEC (2.5%)
Misc. Plastic Products (2.4%)
Dairy Products (2.3%)
Agricultural Products—Crops (2.2%)
Glass and Glass Products (2.0%)
Manufactured Goods (not specified) (1.8%)

3.3% reported carrying beverages, 3.0% were carrying meat products, 2.3% were carrying dairy products, and 2.2% were carrying agricultural crops. Furniture and fixtures accounted for 3.3% of shipments, and lumber and sawmill products made up 3.2% of shipments. Manufactured goods were also important. Nonelectric machinery not elsewhere specified accounted for 2.5% of shipments, while unspecified manufactured goods made up 1.8% of shipments. Miscellaneous plastic products comprised 2.4% of shipments, while glass and glass products comprised 2.0% of shipments.

Demographics

Where Our Respondents Lived

Given the region in which the survey was administered, it is no surprise that half of the sample (49.8%) reported living or having a domicile point in the East North Central states—Illinois, Indiana, Michigan, Ohio, and Wisconsin. The second-largest group of drivers, 15.2%, was from the states that the Institute for Social Research terms the Solid South—Alabama, Arkansas, Florida, Georgia, Louisiana, Mississippi, North Carolina, South Carolina, Texas, and Virginia. The third-largest group, 11.6% of respondents, was from the Border States of Kentucky, Maryland, Oklahoma, Tennessee, the District of Columbia, and West Virginia. Interviews with drivers indicated that the large portion of drivers from the Solid South may be due to the low wage scale in that region. The low wages that have historically characterized many industries in this region make the earnings of drivers more attractive than they would be elsewhere in the country.

Age

Truck drivers tend to be older than other blue-collar workers. Few of those who responded to the driver survey were under 21 (0.7%). In contrast, 6.75% of the national blue-collar sample are between the ages 18 and 20. Although employees between ages 21 and 24 are legally able to drive trucks, only 2.2% of the driver labor force falls between these ages.

■ Figure 3. Residence of Respondents

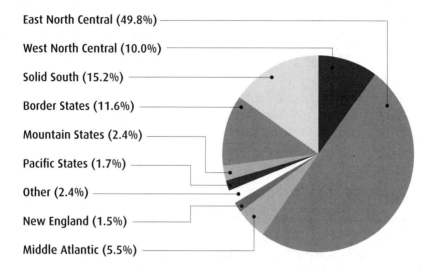

East North Central (49.8%)
West North Central (10.0%)
Solid South (15.2%)
Border States (11.6%)
Mountain States (2.4%)
Pacific States (1.7%)
Other (2.4%)
New England (1.5%)
Middle Atlantic (5.5%)

Somewhat more than nine percent (9.4%) of the national blue-collar sample is between 21 and 24. The proportion of drivers aged 25 to 34 is closer to that of the national sample, 21.8% and 25.2%, respectively. This pattern reverses itself between ages 35 and 54. A larger proportion of the driver labor force than the national blue-collar work force is between ages 35 and 44, 36.7% compared to 26.9%. The same holds for ages 45 to 54, with 27.2% of the driver labor force but only 20.4% of the blue-collar labor force falling within this age group. The proportion of employees 55 and older is similar for the two groups.

The difference in the age distribution is, in part, attributable to legal limits on the age at which workers can drive commercial trucks. Drivers in interstate commerce are required to hold a Commercial Driver's License (CDL) and the license is available only to those 21 and older. Yet this is not a complete explanation. The cost of tractor-trailers, the value of the cargo, and the lack of immediate supervision may disincline firms from hiring young, potentially immature workers. Another factor may be an inability of younger employees to obtain the funds required to become

■ Table 3. Age of Drivers Compared to National Blue-Collar Sample

| | NATIONAL BLUE-COLLAR | DRIVER SURVEY | | |
| | | ALL DRIVERS | EMPLOYEES | OWNER-OPERATORS* |
AGE	SAMPLE (CPS)		UNION	NONUNION	(NONUNION)
18 to 20	6.7%	0.7%	0.0%	1.0%	0.0%
21 to 24	9.4%	2.2%	1.0%	2.8%	1.3%
25 to 34	25.3%	21.8%	6.7%	24.5%	21.4%
35 to 44	26.9%	36.7%	40.3%	36.8%	35.6%
45 to 54	20.4%	27.2%	38.8%	26.8%	22.2%
55 to 64	9.0%	9.7%	12.3%	6.7%	16.2%
65 to 74	2.1%	1.7%	0.9%	1.1%	3.3%
75 or more	0.3%	0.1%	0.0%	0.2%	0.0%

Note: All statistics are calculated with weights proportional to probability of appearing in sample.
*Does not include two owner-operators who are union members.

■ Figure 4. Age of Driver Workforce Compared to National Blue-Collar Sample

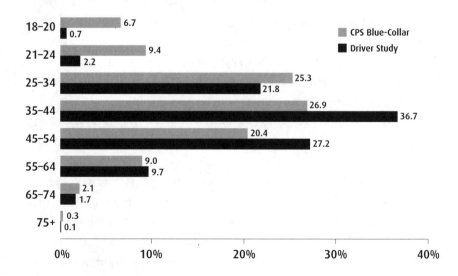

an owner-operator. Although these factors increase the importance of prime age males in the trucking labor force, it does not appear that truck drivers are more likely to continue working in their occupation after age 54 than men in other blue-collar occupations.

There are conspicuous differences in the age distribution of union employees, nonunion employees, and nonunion owner-operators. Nonunion employees are the youngest: 24.5% are between 25 and 34, 36.8% are between 35 and 44, and 26.8% are between 45 and 54. Only 6.7% of nonunion employees are between 55 and 64. Union employees are considerably older, on average. Only 6.7% are between 25 and 34, while 40.3% are 35 to 44, 38.8% are 45 to 54, and 12.3%, nearly twice the proportion of nonunion employees, are 55 to 64. The number of nonunion owner-operators falls below that of either union or nonunion employees for ages 25 to 54, but owner-operators are the most likely to be 55 to 64 (16.2%), or older (3.3%). The need for capital and the ability to pace one's work may explain the larger proportion of this older group among owner-operators.[6]

Sex

Driving is a male-dominated profession. Of our respondents, 97.2% of drivers were men, and only 2.8% were women. This contrasts with the national blue-collar sample provided in the *1997 Outgoing Rotation File of the U.S. Bureau of Labor Statistics,* in which 60.2% of the sample was male and 39.8% was female.[7] Interviews with drivers indicated that the need to be away from home for extended periods makes the job unattractive to women with families. Those women in the sample tended to be older women whose children were already grown. In view of the small proportion of women in the driver labor force, the balance of survey's benchmark data on the blue-collar labor force is limited to a male sample.

Race and Ethnicity

Drivers were asked to classify their race and whether they were Hispanic. The racial distribution of the driver labor force is similar to that of the male blue-collar labor force. More than eighty-five percent (85.3%) of drivers reported they were white, 8.9% reported being African American, 1.8% reported being Native American, and 4.1% fell into other classifications. For the blue-collar labor force as a whole, 83.1% are white, 12.8% are African American, 0.8% are Native American, and 3.3% are Asian American or other. Differences in the racial composition of the drivers in this survey and the national blue collar labor force are explained by differences in the regional distribution of racial groups. For example, there are fewer African Americans in the Midwest than in the national sample, which includes the South.

The issue of Hispanic origin and ethnicity is distinct from that of race. Hispanics make up a smaller proportion of the driver sample, specifically 2.0%, than they do of the national sample, where Hispanics comprise 8.5% of the national male blue-collar workforce. Again, this difference is explained by regional differences in the distribution of Hispanic workers.

Educational Attainment

Drivers typically have less formal education than other male blue collar workers. In excess of sixty percent (64.3%) of drivers completed their education with no more than a high school degree, this group comprised only slightly over half (51.3%) of all male blue collar workers. A larger proportion of drivers than male blue collar workers ended their education with a high school degree (43.7% and 32.5%, respectively). Drivers are also more likely to have attended of high school without earning a degree; 18.3% entered high school without graduating compared to 6.7% of all male blue collar workers. Only a small proportion of either group did not enter high school: 2.3% of drivers compared to 2.1% of blue collar workers.

Slightly more than one-third of drivers (35.8%) have education beyond high school. Almost one-quarter attended college but did not earn a degree (22.7%), 4.4% earned a vocational degree or completed an apprenticeship program, 3.9% earned an associate's (two-year) degree and 4.8% hold a bachelor's (four-year) degree. The proportion of male

■ Table 4. Characteristics of Respondents

ITEM		DRIVER SURVEY	NATIONAL BLUE-COLLAR SAMPLE (CPS)
Sex	Male	97.2%	60.2%
	Female	2.8%	39.8%
Race	White	85.3%	83.1%
	African American	8.9%	12.8%
	Native American	1.8%	0.8%
	Other	4.1%	3.3%
Ethnicity	Hispanic	2.0%	8.5%
Educational Attainment	Less than High School	2.3%	2.1%
	Some High School	18.3%	6.7%
	High School Degree	43.7%	32.5%
	Some College	22.7%	21.8%
	Vocational Degree	4.4%	5.3%
	Associate Degree	3.9%	4.6%
	Four-Year Degree or More	4.8%	27.1%
Marital Status	Never Married	12.8%	26.4%
	Married	63.6%	54.5%
	Separated	4.1%	3.4%
	Divorced	17.0%	12.5%
	Widowed	2.6%	3.2%
Number of Children	0	41.4%	61.2%
	1	21.4%	16.7%
	2	22.1%	15.1%
	3	8.9%	5.3%
	4	4.2%	1.1%
	5	1.5%	0.5%
	6 or more	0.5%	0.2%

National blue-collar sample taken from 1997 CPS and April 1993 Benefits supplement to the CPS. Except for data on sex, CPS data is limited to male blue-collar workers age 21 and older.

■ Figure 5. Educational Attainment of Driver Workforce Compared to National Blue-Collar Sample

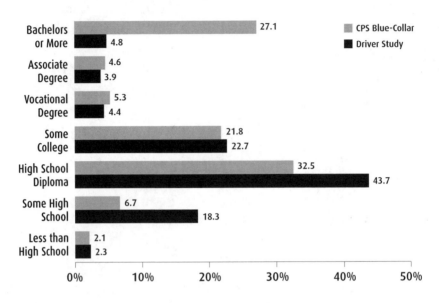

blue-collar workers reporting some college, vocational and associate degrees is close that that reported by drivers, but male blue-collar workers are considerably more likely to have completed a four year degree (27.1%).

Marriage and Children

Truck drivers are inclined toward traditional families. They are more likely to be married and to have more children than the typical male blue-collar worker.[8] Driver survey data shows that 63.6% of drivers are married, compared to 54.5% of the national blue-collar sample. Drivers are less likely to have never been married (12.8% for drivers compared to 26.4% for the national sample), or divorced (17.0% vs. 12.5%), but are slightly more likely to be separated. Drivers also have more children than the typical male blue-collar worker. Drivers are less likely to have no children (41.4% compared to 61.2%), and more likely to have one (21.4%/16.7%), two (22.1%/15.1%), three (8.9%/5.3%), or more children (6.2%/1.8%) than the typical male blue-collar worker.

How Our Respondents Learned to Drive Trucks

Most respondents learned to drive through informal means rather than through a school or other formal program. The largest single source of training was on-the-job experience, with 43.8% of drivers reporting they learned on the job. Informal training was also reported as provided by family members or neighbors (12.0%). One-quarter of drivers obtained their initial training from private driving schools (18.7%) or from public technical schools (8.6%). Such programs promise to prepare students to pass the commercial drivers license (CDL) examination after three to four weeks of training. Other important sources of experience are trucking company programs (6.5%) and the military (6.0%). The training provided by the largest trucking firms starts with several weeks of classroom/day trip experience, which is then followed by several months of over-the-road driving with a more experienced driver.

The pattern of informal training or limited formal training allows

■ Figure 6. Sources of Driver Training

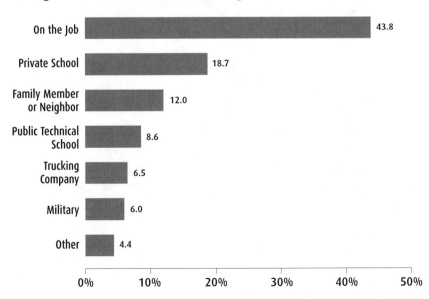

easy entry into the occupation, although entry is somewhat restricted by the requirements of the CDL. Easy entry has been an important feature of the occupation and does much to determine the nature of the work and characteristics of the workforce. Small increases in earnings can quickly draw in new entrants and restrain any further increase in earnings. Easy entry and the lack of extended training may also be a source of poor driving habits, such as drivers' reported failure to recognize the need for adequate sleep.

CHAPTER 2

Driving Distances and Earnings

Data on the pay and earnings of truck drivers is scarce. Although large national data sets such as the Current Population Survey ask about drivers' weekly earnings, hourly rates, and hours of work, these questions are sufficiently at variance with how drivers are paid and how they report their time to circumscribe the usefulness of this data.

Truck drivers, however, are not typically paid by the hour and do not report working hours as would most employees. Although our data set indicates that 10% of drivers are paid by the hour, most are paid mileage rates, a fixed rate per mile driven, or as a percentage of the revenue earned from a load. Pay for nondriving activities and bonus payments can also comprise a substantial portion of pay. Conversion of such pay systems to statements about weekly or monthly pay is not straightforward. The problem of calculating hourly rates is made more difficult by drivers' tendency to consider driving time as working time and to not report nondriving work, such as loading and unloading or waiting time. Given incongruities between how drivers are paid and how their pay is reported in national data, there is considerable danger of inaccuracy. Furthermore, even if the national figures are accurate, they are not in a form that is useful to drivers or to the industry.

The driver survey asked a series of questions on pay and earnings. Drivers were asked about how they were paid for driving and their rate under that system. They were also asked about pay for nondriving duties, whether they were eligible for bonus payments, and about their annual earnings from trucking. Owner-operators were asked their gross and net earnings from their work. In combination with information about hours of work and mileage collected by the survey, this has allowed us to develop a complete picture that makes it possible to compare driver pay systems with one another and with national wage standards.

The discussion begins with annual mileage and the details of how drivers are paid for driving time. Estimates of the drivers' hourly rates for driving time are also obtained. The next part of the discussion considers pay for nondriving duties, as well as bonus rates. This is followed by a discussion of benefits coverage. Annual income is the next topic, and this information is then combined with the data on annual mileage to calculate a comprehensive mileage rate for all drivers. This rate, called the effective mileage rate, includes all earnings from trucking, including pay for nondriving time and bonuses, and it can be accurately compared across pay systems. We also calculate the effective hourly rate of drivers, a rate that can be compared to the hourly rate of nondriver employees.

Annual Mileage

Respondents were asked how many miles they had driven in 1996, the year immediately before the survey. For the full sample, drivers averaged 109,965, while the median respondent drove 110,000 miles. There was considerable diversity in mileage. Ten percent of respondents drove fewer than 50,000 miles and 25% drove less than 82,000 miles in 1996. A quarter of the sample reported driving 130,000 miles or more in 1996, and 10% of the sample drove 160,000 miles or more.[1] Some of the lower-mileage figures could be the result of drivers entering the workforce midway through 1996. Limiting the sample to drivers with two or more years in the occupation increased average mileage by 4,000 miles.

Dividing the data by employment relationship, union employees reported the lowest annual mileage, with 103,016 miles at the mean and

■ Table 5. Mileage in 1996 by Type of Employment

	ALL	EMPLOYMENT RELATIONSHIP		OWNER-OPERATORS	TYPE OF DRIVER	
		EMPLOYEES			LOCAL	OTR
		UNION	NONUNION	(NONUNION)		
Observations	522	48	325	146	61	461
Annual Mileage						
Mean	109,965	103,016	111,726	108,545	70,176	116,586
10th Percentile	50,000	50,000	50,000	60,000	10,000	65,000
25th Percentile	82,000	80,000	87,000	80,000	30,000	100,000
Median	110,000	100,000	115,000	110,000	70,000	117,000
75th Percentile	130,000	120,000	135,000	130,000	110,000	140,000
90th Percentile	160,000	150,000	160,000	158,000	125,000	162,000

Note: Individuals reporting 0 miles or more than 350,000 miles in 1996 were not included in these calculations.

■ Figure 7. Mileage in 1996 by Type of Employment

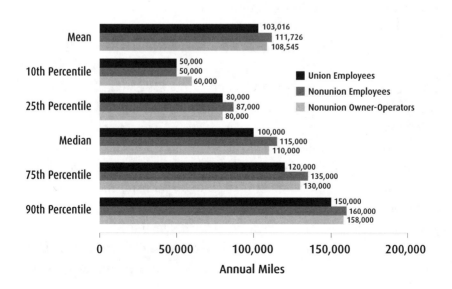

100,000 at the median. Nonunion owner-operators drove slightly more, 108,545 and 110,000 at the mean and median, respectively. Nonunion employees reported driving the most miles, with a mean of 111,726 and a median of 115,000 miles a year. Over-the-road drivers put in more miles than local drivers. Mean annual mileage for over-the-road drivers is 116,586, versus 70,176 for local drivers. Median mileage for these groups is 117,000 and 70,000, respectively. This difference reflects the diversity of the jobs, with local drivers spending more time on nondriving work, such as loading and unloading. (Further details are presented in the section on hours of work.)

Including on-duty nondriving time, the average speed of a trip is thirty-seven miles per hour (see chapter 6). A driver who averaged thirty-seven miles per hour and drove sixty hours per week, fifty weeks per year, would drive 111,300 miles annually. Our typical respondent is then working close to three thousand hours annually to drive his or her reported mileage. This is consistent with the weekly hours of work and time off reported by our respondents.

Pay Systems for Driving Time

Most drivers are paid by the mile (55.8%) or by percentage of revenue (30%). Pay by the hour is less common, with fewer than 10% of the sample reporting hourly rates for driving time.

Mileage rates were the most common payment scheme for both union (51.9%) and nonunion (63.0%) employees. Nearly thirty-eight percent (37.7%) of nonunion owner-operators are paid mileage rates. It is also the dominant pay scheme for over-the-road drivers, with nearly 71% being paid by the mile. Pay by the mile provides a strong incentive to the driver to complete dispatches expeditiously. This fits shippers' and dispatchers' desire to get loads to their destinations as quickly as is feasible (see the chapter on log books). In an industry in which people in the Midwest want their produce from California in two days, mileage pay ensures that drivers strive to meet such demands.

Although less than one-third of drivers are paid a percentage of revenue, it is the most common payment system among nonunion owner-

■ Table 6. Systems and Rates of Compensation on Current Trip

| | ALL | EMPLOYMENT RELATIONSHIP | | OWNER-OPERATORS | TYPE OF DRIVER | | |
| | | EMPLOYEES | | | LOCAL | OTR EMPLOYEE | OTR OWNER-OPERATOR |
		UNION	NONUNION	(NONUNION)			
Observations	520	44	341	133	51	334	124
Mileage (% of sample)							
	55.8%	51.9%	63.0%	37.7%	12.7%	70.9%	37.9%
Mileage Rates (cents per mile)							
Mean		48.4	28.4	97.1	33.7	30.7	94.2
10th Percentile		25	23	80	✶	23	80
25th Percentile		32	25	80	✶	25	80
Median		37	28	84	34	28	82
75th Percentile		45	30	105	✶	31	95
90th Percentile		94	33	140	✶	36	120
Percent of Revenue (% of sample)							
	29.9%	17.3%	22.6%	55.7%	27.8%	20.3%	57.8%
Revenue Rates							
Mean		✶	28.1%	71.9%	34.4%	26.0%	72.0%
10th Percentile		✶	22%	61%	✶	21%	61%
25th Percentile		✶	23%	66%	✶	23%	67%
Median		✶	25%	74%	29%	25%	74%
75th Percentile		✶	29%	75%	✶	27%	75%
90th Percentile		✶	45%	82%	✶	30%	82%
Hourly (% of sample)							
	10.0%	30.9%	9.4%	2.2%	48.8%	5.6%	0.0%
Hourly Rates (dollars per hour)							
Mean	13.50	15.60	12.32	✶	12.60	15.00	✶
Median	13.00	15.50	12.15	✶	11.70	14.00	✶

Notes: The hourly rates were trimmed, with those reporting less than 0.22 and greater than 52 eliminated. Drivers who reported multiple pay schemes for their driving time were not included in the above calculations. The mileage rate and percentage revenue reported by owner-operators are not directly comparable to those reported by employees, since they implicitly include the cost of the tractor.

*Not reported due to small sample size.

■ Figure 8. Systems of Compensation by Type of Employment

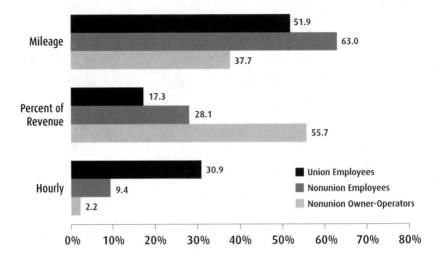

operators. Such systems are less common among employees, with 17.3% of nonunion employees and 22.6% of union employees being paid by percentage of revenue. Payment as a percentage of revenue pays according to the value of the shipment and so adjusts the driver's share according to the payment to the broker or trucking firm. Some respondents noted that they were unsure that their employers were reporting the revenue associated with the loads correctly. Others believed that firms gave low-revenue loads to those being paid a percentage of revenue, thereby shifting losses onto the driver.

Hourly rates are most common among union employees, with 30.9% reporting hourly rates for driving. Only 2.2% of owner-operators and 9.4% of nonunion employees are paid in this manner. Local drivers spend more of their time on nondriving work, and hourly pay systems fit their duties better than they do those of over-the-road drivers. Dividing the respondents by type of work, only 5.6% of over-the-road employees and no (0%) over-the-road owner-operators are paid hourly. In contrast, 48.8% of local drivers report being paid hourly for driving time. The high proportion of union employees paid by the hour is due, in part, to the high proportion of union drivers who work in the local driving market.

Mileage Rates

Mileage rates vary considerably between owner-operators and employees, as payments to owner-operators include truck expenses as well as labor. The earnings advantage or disadvantage of owner-operators depends upon the per-mile cost of operating the truck. Separating the labor and truck payments requires some calculation, so we first turn to the simpler issue of mileage rates for employees.

The mean mileage rate of union employees is $0.48 cents per mile, approximately 40% higher than that of nonunion employees—$0.28 cents per mile. The median rates are less disparate, $0.37 and $0.28, respectively, with a 32% union rate advantage. The difference between the mean and median mileage rates of union employees (not seen in nonunion employees) suggests that some union employees are earning

■ Figure 9. Rates of Compensation by Type of Employment

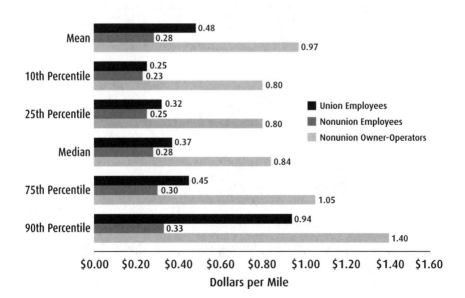

high mileage rates. Indeed, 25% of union employees earn $0.45 and higher and 10% earn $0.94 per mile and higher. This contrasts sharply with nonunion employees, whose corresponding figures are $0.30 and $0.33.

Owner-operators earn higher mileage rates, but part of this payment is for truck expenses and depreciation. The mean payment is $0.97 per mile, and the median is ten cents lower, at $0.84 per mile. Less than 10% of drivers report rates of less than $0.80 per mile, 25% of the owner-operators report earning at least $1.05 per mile, and 10% report earning at least $1.40 per mile. Comparison of these rates to those of employees requires distinguishing the payment for the equipment from the payment for labor. Data from drivers who are paid a percentage of revenue indicate that 60% to 66% of the payment to owner-operators goes to the truck. Using this ratio, owner-operators' labor earnings are between $0.29 and $0.34 per mile at the median, somewhat above those of nonunion employees but below those of union employees.

Local drivers have a slight advantage in their mean wage, $0.34 per miles versus $0.31 for over-the-road employees. This advantage is larger at the median, with local drivers earning $0.34 versus $0.28 for over-the-road employees. This pay advantage reflects the higher rate of organization of local drivers and the need to provide reasonable weekly earnings to local drivers, who drive fewer miles than over-the-road drivers.

Over-the-road drivers average 37.1 miles per hour while on duty (see chapter 6) and this can be used to convert mileage rates into hourly rates. Union employees earn $17.97 per hour of driving time, nonunion employees earn $10.53, and nonunion owner-operators earn $35.17 gross and $12.61 net of truck expenses per hour.

Percentage of Revenue

As with mileage rates, there are substantial differences between percentage of revenue rates for employees and owner-operators. At the mean, nonunion employees are paid 28% of the revenue from the load, and owner-operators are paid 72%. This differential is larger at the median, with employees earning 25% and owner-operators earning

■ **Figure 10. Percent of Revenue of Nonunion Employees and Nonunion Owner-Operators**

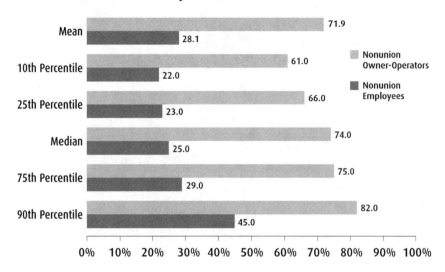

74% of revenue.[2] Few local employees are paid a percentage of revenue; those who are receive rates comparable to the rates of over-the-road employees (29% versus 25% for over-the-road). At the mean this difference is slightly higher, with local drivers at 34% and over-the-road employees at 26%. This data is not readily converted into dollar values or into mileage or hourly rates. Drivers' earnings will vary with the revenue associated with a load, and this may vary considerably both between loads and between respondents. As a result, there is no straightforward association between the percentage of revenue earned and dollar earnings.

Hourly Rates

Hourly rates are the second-most common pay scheme for union employees, with 31% paid hourly. The mean and median hourly rates are similar, at $15.60 and $15.50, respectively. The average hourly rate for nonunion employees is $12.32, while the median is $12.15 per hour. Owner-operators are excluded from the analysis, as only 2.2% report

■ **Figure 11. Hourly Rates of Compensation of Union Employees and Nonunion Employees**

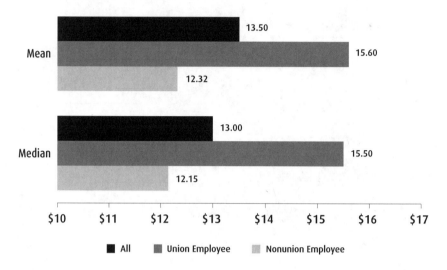

being paid by the hour for their driving time. Local drivers are more likely to be paid by the hour for their driving time than are over-the-road employees, and 49% are paid by the hour. The mean hourly wage of local drivers is $12.60 and the median is $11.70. These rates are only slightly lower than those calculated for over-the-road drivers who are nonunion employees, a result that is sensible, given the similarity of the jobs and skills and the permeability of the labor markets for local and over-the-road drivers.

Nondriving Time: Working and Waiting

Although the majority of respondents' time was spent driving, 20% of the driver's workday was devoted to nondriving duties (see the chapter on hours of work). The typical driver works three thousand hours per year, and spends six hundred of these hours on nondriving work.

To develop a more complete portrait of drivers' work lives, respondents were asked detailed questions about on-duty nondriving time and

■ Table 7. Nondriving Compensation: Working and Waiting

	ALL	EMPLOYMENT RELATIONSHIP		OWNER-OPERATORS	TYPE OF DRIVER		
		EMPLOYEES			LOCAL	OTR EMPLOYEE	OTR OWNER-OPERATOR
		UNION	NONUNION	(NONUNION)			
	573	50	369	151	56	363	142

Working. *Are you paid for . . .*
loading and unloading?

| | 44.7% | 64.4% | 46.0% | 34.0% | 59.2% | 46.8% | 33.3% |

dropping and hooking?

| | 21.2% | 46.0% | 22.9% | 5.9% | 46.9% | 22.3% | 6.5% |

| other work? | 10.6% | 20.7% | 9.9% | 8.4% | 15.2% | ˙10.8% | 8.5% |

Waiting. *Are you paid for waiting . . .*
to be loaded and unloaded?

| | 32.6% | 68.8% | 30.0% | 23.9% | 59.9% | 31.1% | 22.6% |

| for a dispatch? | 24.1% | 46.9% | 24.6% | 12.2% | 45.4% | 24.5% | 12.3% |
| for anything else? | 13.8% | 33.5% | 13.7% | 5.0% | 18.7% | 16.3% | 4.7% |

their pay for such work on the last completed trip. Such work is reasonably divided between waiting tasks, which require the driver to be available but do not require physical exertion, and working tasks. The former include waiting for loading or unloading or waiting for a dispatch. The latter include work such as loading, unloading, dropping, hooking, and tarping. Hours spent performing these tasks are summarized in the chapter on hours of work. This chapter focuses on pay for these tasks.

Working tasks are demanding, especially loading and unloading. Drivers may be asked to move thirty thousand pounds of goods, often under conditions in which forklifts are unavailable or cannot be used. Nearly forty-five percent (44.7%) of all drivers reported that they were paid when they loaded or unloaded trucks. Forty-one percent of those who had loaded or unloaded a truck on the last trip had been paid for that activity. Pay for unloading is common among union employees, with 64.4% reporting being paid for such work. It is less common for nonunion employees, with only 46.0% being paid, and least common for owner-operators with 34.0% being paid.[3]

The pattern for dropping and hooking the trailer is similar. Of those who reported spending time dropping and hooking on their last trip, 21.2% had been paid for this activity. Union employees are most likely to be paid for dropping and hooking, with 46.0% receiving pay for this duty. Owner-operators are the least likely to be paid, with 5.9% reporting pay for dropping and hooking, while 22.9% of nonunion employees are paid for this work.

Nearly eleven percent (10.6%) of drivers reported being paid for some other type of work. Almost twenty-one percent (20.7%) of union employees are paid for other types of work, 9.9% of nonunion employees are paid for other work, and only 8.4% of nonunion owner-operators reported such payments. What is this other work? Truck maintenance is the most frequent. Of those reporting pay for other work, 20% are paid for maintenance. Tarping is the second-most common (11%), and residential delivery the third (8%).

The distinction between waiting time as work time and as rest time is ambiguous. Our interviews indicated that drivers may take breaks or sleep during waiting time, and that they often do not count such time as work time. Although drivers may be able to rest or nap during some of the waiting time, they also report that short breaks and the need for drivers to be available on short notice—such as when a loading dock clears—limits the effectiveness of rest time taken while waiting. Waiting time is less likely to be paid than work time. Only about one-third of drivers, (32.6%) had received pay for time spent waiting while their truck was loaded or unloaded on their last trip. In addition, 24.1% of drivers had been paid for waiting for a dispatch, and 13.8% had been paid for waiting for other reasons. Of these, 18.3% had been paid for truck breakdowns, 17.7% for layovers, and 5.1% for waiting to get into a dock. When waiting time was paid, paid time often began only after an initial waiting period of four to twenty-four hours had elapsed. This was particularly characteristic of nonunion employees and owner-operators.

Again, union drivers are more often compensated for their waiting time than are nonunion drivers. Nearly sixty-nine percent (68.8%) of union drivers are paid for waiting to be loaded or unloaded, 46.9% are paid for waiting for a dispatch, and 33.5% are paid for waiting for other reasons. Thirty percent of nonunion employees are paid if they have to wait to be loaded or unloaded, 24.6% are paid when they wait for a dispatch, and 13.7% of nonunion employees report being paid to wait for other reasons. Only 23.9% of owner-operators are paid while waiting for loading and unloading, 12.2% are paid while waiting for a dispatch, and 5.0% are paid for other forms of waiting time.

There is an incentive for drivers to record unpaid waiting time as breaks or as off-duty time. Drivers are limited to fifteen hours of work prior to an eight hour break, and substantial waiting periods may reduce the total working time and driving time available to the driver. Recording such unpaid time as off-duty preserves working time, even if it extends the effective workday beyond its legal limit.

Bonus Payments

Bonus schemes serve to reward and thereby encourage behaviors desired by their employers. The survey asked whether respondents' firms had programs that compensated employees for on-time performance or for good safety records.[4] Nearly forty percent (39.6%) of drivers reported that the firm they worked for offered a safety bonus. This bonus was more common among nonunion employees (47.8%) than among union employees (26.8%) or owner-operators (25.2%). Safety bonuses are important to firms for obvious reasons: the equipment and the load are valuable, the direct and indirect costs of accidents can be quite high, and accidents can damage the reputation of a firm.

Payment for on-time performance is consonant with the concerns of trucking firms and shippers (see the chapter on log books). With dispatchers unable to closely monitor drivers, pay supplements for on-time performance ensure that drivers have the incentive to accommodate these concerns. Nearly twenty-two percent (21.8%) of respondents

■ Figure 12. Bonus Payments by Type of Employment

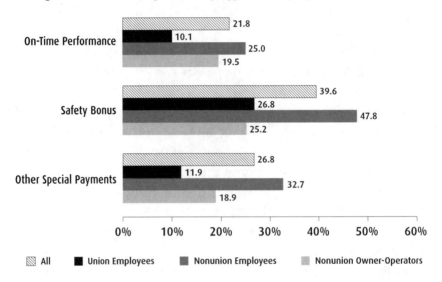

■ Figure 13. Other Special Payments of All Drivers

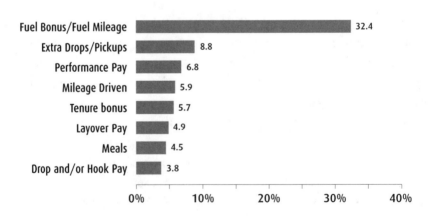

receive extra payments for on-time performance. Not surprisingly, such payments are more common among nonunion employees (25.0%) and owner-operators (19.5%) than among union employees (10.1%).

An additional 26.8% of drivers reported that their firms offered other special payments for driving. More than thirty-two percent (32.4%)

of these respondents received a fuel bonus. Bonuses for performance, for mileage, and for remaining with the firm were also common.

Benefits

Benefits such as pensions, health insurance, holidays, and vacation time have become an increasingly important component of employee compensation over the last four decades. Nationally such benefits account for about 20% of the total cost of employment (Mishel, Bernstein, and Schmitt 1999, 137). The most prominent and costly benefits are health insurance and retirement income. Retirement income plans are complex, but may be divided into three types: conventional pension plans, which have structured payouts typically based on age and years of service and which provide lifetime income after retirement; deferred compensation plans, such as profit sharing or other plans that accumulate

■ **Figure 14. Compensation, Retirement, and Insurance by Type of Employment**

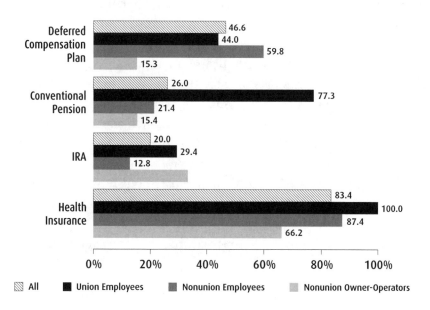

amounts specific to the plan holder and provide a fixed amount to the plan holder on retirement; and IRA or Keogh plans, which are established by individuals. Drivers were asked whether they participated in each type of plan and, if they did, were asked about the source and funding of the plan. Drivers were also asked about vacation time, holiday time, and sick leave, with regard to both the number of days taken and the number of days paid.

Health Insurance Plans

Most drivers had some form of health insurance. Nearly eighty-three percent (83.4%) of respondents reported participating in a health insurance plan. All union employees reported coverage. Health insurance coverage was also very high among nonunion employees, with 87.4% reporting participation. Owner-operators were the least likely to have health insurance, with only about two-thirds (66.2%) reporting coverage.

Most employees received their insurance through their employer or union. Ninety-two percent of union employees and 86.5% of nonunion employees with health coverage reported that their coverage was through their employer. In contrast, only 20.9% of owner-operators with health insurance received it through a company or union, while 46.6% had purchased the insurance from private sources and 23.2% received health insurance through their spouse.

Who pays for health insurance? Among union employees, 53.2% reported that their employer paid the full cost, 41.3% reported that their employer paid part of the cost, and 5.6% reported that their firm paid none of the cost. Nonunion employees are more likely to pay part of the cost of health insurance. Only 27.4% reported that their employer paid the full cost, 58.1% reported that their employer paid part of the cost, and 14.6% reported that their employer paid none of the cost. Employers seldom pay any part of the cost of owner-operators' health insurance: 75.5% reported no employer contribution, 16.3% reported some contribution, and only 8.2% reported that the employer paid the full cost.

■ Table 8. Benefits: Compensation, Retirement, and Insurance

	ALL DRIVERS	EMPLOYEES		OWNER-OPERATORS
		UNION	NONUNION	(NONUNION)
Do you have . . .	572	50	369	151
deferred compensation plan?	46.6%	44.0%	59.8%	15.3%
through company/union	92.6%	100.0%	96.7%	41.0%
company pays: all	16.6%	17.4%	17.6%	2.8%
part	64.7%	52.0%	68.7%	40.1%
none	18.7%	30.6%	13.5%	57.2%
conventional pension?	26.0%	77.3%	21.4%	15.4%
source: company/union	67.5%	95.7%	63.2%	18.0%
military	5.7%	0.0%	4.2%	24.4%
other	26.8%	4.3%	32.6%	57.6%
IRA?	20.0%	29.4%	12.8%	33.3%
health insurance?	83.4%	100.0%	87.4%	66.2%
source*: company/union	74.2%	92.0%	86.5%	20.9%
spouse	12.1%	9.9%	9.3%	23.2%
private purchase	13.6%	7.0%	5.0%	46.6%
company pays: all	27.4%	53.2%	27.4%	8.2%
part	48.1%	41.3%	58.1%	16.3%
none	24.5%	5.6%	14.6%	75.5%

*Percentages may not sum to 100 due to multiple policies from different sources.

Conventional Pensions

Conventional pensions are less common among truck drivers than they were twenty years ago. This reflects not only changes in the structure of pensions throughout the workforce but also the limitations of conventional pension systems for industries in which there is rapid turnover and limited portability outside of the organized sector.

Conventional pensions are largely restricted to the organized sector. More than three-quarters of union employees (77.3%) report participating in a conventional pension scheme. In contrast, about one-fifth of nonunion employees (21.4%) and less than one-sixth of owner-operators (15.4%) report having a conventional pension. Although nearly all union employees' pensions are provided by their employers and unions, only 63.2% of nonunion employees with pensions and 18.0% of owner-operators with pensions have their pensions through their employers. Nearly one-quarter of owner-operators with pensions receive those pensions through the military.

Deferred Compensation Plans: 401(k)s and IRAs

The majority of those with a deferred compensation plan participate in 401(k) plans provided by their employer. Almost half of the respondents report participation in such plans, and they are particularly common among nonunion employees (59.8%). A substantial proportion of union employees (44.0%) also participate in deferred compensation plans, but few owner-operators report participation (15.3%). Almost all of the deferred compensation plans are provided through employers. The exception to this is owner-operators. Only 41% of owner-operators with plans obtain their plan from their employer, the firm to whom they lease. Most plans have shared funding: 64.7% of respondents report that their firm pays part of the cost of the plan, while 16.6% report that the firm pays the full cost, and 18.7% report that the firm pays none of the cost of the plan. Shared funding is most common among nonunion employees (68.7%). About half of union participants (52.0%) also report shared funding. Fewer owner-operators (40.1%) have shared funding, and 57.2% of owner-operators with deferred compensation plans receive no funds from their employer.

Another form of saving for retirement is an Individual Retirement Account. These are less common among drivers than are conventional pensions or a deferred compensation plan; only one in five drivers has

■ Table 9. Benefits: Vacations, Holidays, and Sick Leave

	ALL DRIVERS	EMPLOYEES		OWNER-OPERATORS
		UNION	NONUNION	(NONUNION)
VACATION: DAYS OF VACATION TAKEN				
Median Days	5	5	5	7
Percent with None Taken	38.7%	28.4%	39.4%	41.8%
VACATION: DAYS OF PAID VACATION				
Median Days	5	10	7	0
Percent with None	34.5%	7.9%	15.7%	92.7%
HOLIDAYS: HOLIDAYS TAKEN				
Median Days	4	6	3	4
Percent with None Taken	19.8%	10.4%	22.1%	18.2%
HOLIDAYS: PAID HOLIDAY TIME				
Median Days	0	7	3	0
Percent with None	52.6%	17.0%	42.0%	94.3%
SICK LEAVE: DAYS OF SICK LEAVE				
Median Days	0	0	0	0
Mean Days	2.2	1.2	2.3	2.4
Percent with None Taken	78.4%	70.4%	80.4%	76.7%
SICK LEAVE: DAYS OF PAID SICK LEAVE				
Median Days	0	4	0	0
Mean Days	1.1	3.5	1.1	0.1
Percent with None	83.6%	44.3%	84.6%	98.7%

such a plan. They are most common among owner-operators, one third (33.3%) of whom report having such a plan. Almost as many union employees (29.4%) report having such plans, but few nonunion employees report having an IRA.

Vacations

Although most drivers receive vacation pay from their employers, drivers tend to take brief vacations, and many drivers do not take them at all. Drivers report a median of five days of paid vacation per year. Union employees receive the most paid vacation time, with ten days at the median. Nonunion employees receive seven days at the median, and owner-operators typically receive no paid vacation. Nearly thirty-five percent (34.5%) of the driver labor force report they have no paid vacation. This is most common among owner-operators, of whom 92.7% report they have no paid vacation. Only 15.7% of nonunion employees and 7.9% of union employees report they receive no paid vacation time.

Owner-operators took the most vacation, a median of seven days. Both union and nonunion employees took a median of five days of vacation. A substantial proportion of drivers, 38.7%, took no vacation. This was most common among owner-operators, of whom 41.8% took no vacation. It was almost as frequent among nonunion employees, of whom 39.4% took no vacation, and less common among union employees, of whom 28.4% reported no vacation days taken.

Holidays

Similar to vacation time, drivers' time off for holidays is limited. The typical driver takes four holidays off work annually, and typically none of those days are paid. Almost twenty percent (19.8%) of drivers took no holiday time off, and 52.6% reported that they received no paid holiday time from their employer.

The pattern of holiday time off and paid days is similar to that of vacation time. Union employees take more holiday time off and have more paid holidays. A lower proportion of union employees failed to take holidays, and few union employees lack some paid holidays. Nonunion employees take few holiday days. They were typically paid for only three holiday days annually and took only these days. Nearly twenty-two percent (22.1%) took no holidays, and 42.0% reported that they had no paid holidays. Owner-operators took four days of holidays, and these days were typically unpaid. Few owner-operators receive holiday pay.

Sick Leave

The drivers interviewed reported few days of absence from work because of illness, with the median driver having taken no sick days in the last year. However, drivers averaged 2.2 days of illness annually, suggesting that when they are too ill to work they remain away from work for an extended period. Drivers at the ninetieth percentile of sick days lost five days to illness, drivers at the ninety-fifth percentile lost ten days to illness, at the ninety-ninth percentile drivers lost thirty days to illness. With the exception of union employees, drivers typically do not receive pay for days on which they are sick. Nearly eighty-four (83.6%) of the sample reported that they did not receive pay when they were absent from work due to sickness.

Work days lost to illness did not vary by type of employee at the median, but union employees averaged almost one day less of sick leave per year than nonunion employees or nonunion owner-operators. In contrast, union employees were more likely to have work days lost to illness. Nearly seventy percent (70.4%) of union employees lost no work days, compared to 80.4% of nonunion employees and 76.7% of nonunion owner-operators.

Paid sick leave is relatively uncommon among nonunion drivers. Although union employees report having four days of paid sick leave per year at the median, nonunion employees report no paid sick leave at the median. Even the union sector has a substantial number of employees without paid sick leave, (44.3%), but this is nearly half the proportion of nonunion employees without paid sick leave (84.6%). Very few owner-operators have paid sick leave—98.7% have none.

Union employees are more likely to have paid coverage and more likely to take relatively short periods of leave from work due to illness. This is consistent with a system that offers both sick leave and good quality medical treatment. In contrast, nonunion employees and owner-operators appear more likely to continue working through less serious health problems, but more likely to suffer from extended health problems that prevent them from working. This is likewise consistent with a system in which employees do not take time off when they are ill unless they have little choice, because they are not paid when they do not work due to illness, and have limited access to health care.

Annual Income

Drivers are concerned about their annual income. Over the course of the more than five hundred long interviews, drivers almost always focused on their annual income but downplayed the hours required to earn that income. Questions on annual income differ somewhat between employees and owner-operators. All respondents were asked about their annual earnings from their work as a driver before taxes. Owner-operators were also asked their gross annual earnings from trucking and their earnings net of truck expenses. Comparisons between employees and owner-operators were made using before-tax annual income for employees and earnings net of truck expenses (but before taxes) for owner-operators.

Drivers' mean earnings were almost $36,000 annually in 1996 dollars; median earnings were $35,000. This was considerably more than the $28,222 earned by the median wage earner in 1996, but similar to the $34,522 earned at the median by the married man whose spouse was not in the labor force (Mishel, Bernstien and Schmitt 1999, 47, 123). The variation in income between drivers was relatively small: 25% of the sample earned less than $26,000 and 25% earned more than $45,000. Union employees earned substantially more than nonunion employees; their mean annual income was $43,165, compared to $35,551 for nonunion employees. Median annual income was $44,000 and $35,000, respectively. At the high end of the income curve, 25% of union employees earned more than $52,500 and 10% earned more than $62,000. For nonunion employees these figures were $44,800 and $52,000.

Owner-operators' gross income was substantially above that of employees, but these figures must be adjusted for truck expenses to make them comparable to employee earnings. Mean gross income was $66,841, and median gross income was $53,000. Once adjusted for truck expenses, the mean was $33,961, and the median was $33,000. With the exception of the ninetieth percentile of the annual earnings distribution,

■ Table 10. Drivers' 1996 Income

| | ALL | EMPLOYEES | | OWNER-OPERATORS | | LOCAL | OTR/E[1] | OTR/O-O[2] |
| | | UNION | NU[3] | (NONUNION) | | | | |
	NET	NET	NET	GROSS	NET	NET	NET	NET
Observations	*495*	*47*	*322*	*127*	*123*	*49*	*320*	*120*
Mean	$35,985	$43,165	$35,551	$66,841	$33,961	$36,883	$36,764	$34,387
10th Percentile	$15,000	$22,000	$20,000	$24,000	$11,000	$15,000	$21,000	$11,000
25th Percentile	$26,000	$35,000	$27,000	$36,000	$20,000	$28,000	$29,000	$21,000
Median	$35,000	$44,000	$35,000	$53,000	$33,000	$40,000	$35,000	$34,000
75th Percentile	$45,000	$52,500	$44,800	$91,000	$46,000	$46,000	$45,000	$46,000
90th Percentile	$53,000	$62,000	$52,000	$120,000	$58,000	$52,000	$53,000	$58,000

Notes: After excluding individuals who reported 0 in 1996, the top and bottom 1% were trimmed for the net income calculations. Less then $1,400 and greater then $86,000 were trimmed. For the gross income for owner-operators the top and bottom 1% were $9,000 and $200,000, respectively.
1. Employee. 2. Owner-Operator. 3. Nonunion

■ Figure 15. Net Income in 1996 by Type of Employment

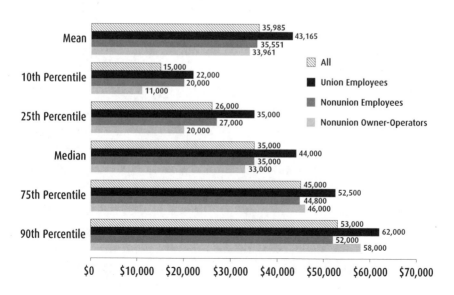

■ Figure 16. Owner-Operators' Income in 1996

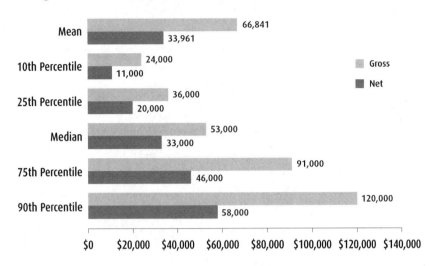

owner-operator earnings were similar to or slightly below those of nonunion employees. The lowest 10% of owner-operators netted $11,000 annually, compared to the $20,000 earned by nonunion employees and the $22,000 earned by union employees. At the high end of the sample, the best off 10% of owner-operators netted $58,000, compared to $52,000 for nonunion employees and the $62,000 earned by the top 10% of union employees.

Two reasons why owner-operators might report earning less than nonunion employees stand out First, owner-operators are less likely to be paid for nondriving time or to receive bonuses. This would reduce their earnings relative to employees. Second, owner-operators have more opportunities than employees to limit their tax liabilities by deducting personal expenses. Trucking lore suggests owner-operators have a liberal attitude toward the deductibility of expenses. This would result in under reporting their net income.

Local drivers' annual earnings are similar to those of over-the-road employees. Both have a mean wage of nearly $37,000. However, there is a disparity in the medians, with local drivers reporting a median of $40,000, compared to $35,000 for over-the-road employees. The gap between the median and mean earnings of local drivers suggests that although the typical local driver earns more than over-the-road drivers, some local drivers work for low wages. Comparison of the lower parts of the earnings distribution confirms this. The tenth percentile of local drivers earn $15,000 annually, compared to the $21,000 in annual earnings for the tenth percentile of over-the-road drivers. At the high end of the pay distribution, the ninetieth percentile of local drivers earned $52,000 in 1996, compared to the $53,000 earned at the ninetieth percentile for over-the-road employees.

As was noted at the beginning of this chapter, the drivers' annual earnings were substantially higher than those of the median wage earner and similar to those of a married couple with a single earner. Both these comparisons suggest that drivers earned a middle-class income. Adjusting the figures for hours of work alters this assessment. In 1996 the median-income employee in the United States earned $28,222 for 1,868 hours' work. In contrast, drivers typically worked 3,000 hours; their mean earnings for 1,869 hours of work would be $22,416, and their median earnings would be $21,800. Drivers are purchasing their middle-class lifestyle by working more than half again the number of hours that the typical employee works.

Another Look at Mileage Rates

The data on annual income and annual mileage can be used to construct an effective mileage rate, to see whether drivers' reported mileage rates and annual incomes agree with each other. In contrast with actual mileage rates, effective mileage rates incorporate payment for driving and nondriving time and all bonuses. The effective rate is also useful because it can be constructed for all drivers, regardless of their pay scheme.

The median effective rate for union employees is 38.4 cents per mile, 1.4 cents more than the median actual rate (table 11). For nonunion employees the effective rate is 31.2 cents, compared to an actual rate of 28.4 cents; for nonunion owner-operators the effective and actual rates are 83.3 and 84.0 cents per mile. The differences in the actual and effective median rates are small and follow an expected pattern. Nonunion employees—employees for whom bonuses are most common and important—have the largest gap between effective and actual rates. Union employees have a much smaller gap. Owner-operators' actual and effective rates are very similar, a result that is predictable for the group that is least likely to receive bonuses or contingent pay.

Comparison of the effective mileage rates of nonunion employees with the net effective mileage rates of nonunion owner-operators indicates that their labor earnings are virtually identical. The medians are within one cent per mile, the means within three cents, and the seventy-fifth and ninetieth percentiles are no more than three cents apart. There is little difference in the rate of pay of nonunion employees and nonunion owner-operators.

Hourly Rates

Tallies of annual earnings and annual hours of work can be used to calculate an hourly rate of pay for drivers. How many hours do drivers work annually? Data presented in chapter 3 (see table 14) suggests that the median driver works sixty hours in seven days. Although there are reasons to believe this is an underestimate, it is an adequate first approximation. How many weeks do drivers typically work annually? Again, our figures indicate that the median driver took five days of vacation, four holiday days, and no sick days (see table 9). The driver labor market has been very tight over the past several years, and the median driver reported no days of unemployment in 1996. Based on this data, the typical driver took two weeks off from work and worked fifty weeks. This suggests a work year of at least 3,000 hours, although there are reasons to believe actual working hours were higher. Annual hours of work vary by type of employee. Union employees work sixty hours per week, but report fifteen days of vacation, holiday time, and sick days, and therefore work 2,940 hours per year. Nonunion employees work sixty-five hours per week and take eight days off, suggesting they work 3,306

Table 11. Ratio of Annual Earnings to Annual Miles

	EMPLOYMENT RELATIONSHIP			
	EMPLOYEES		OWNER-OPERATORS	
	UNION	NONUNION	(NONUNION)	
			GROSS	NET
Observations	*47*	*304*	*110*	*101*
Mileage Rates *(cents per mile)*				
Mean	44.6	37.9	90.9	35.2
10th Percentile	20.0	20.0	28.1	15.0
25th Percentile	30.6	24.7	47.4	20.0
Median	38.4	31.2	83.3	32.7
75th Percentile	53.0	41.5	105.9	43.6
90th Percentile	68.0	60.0	140.4	60.0

hours annually. Owner-operators work the fewest hours annually. They take eleven days off and work fifty-six hours per week at the median, resulting in 2,824 annual hours of work.

With a median annual income of $35,000, the typical driver earned $11.67 per hour worked. Union employees earned the highest rates, at $14.68 per hour; nonunion employees earned $10.75 per hour of work, and nonunion owner-operators earned $12.03 per hour. The median hourly wage for all workers in the private economy in 1996 was $14.29, and the hourly wage of male blue-collar workers was $12.07 (Mishel, Bernstein, and Schmitt 1999, 126–29). Although union employees earn substantially more than typical blue-collar employees, owner-operators' hourly earnings are close to those of blue-collar workers, and nonunion employees earn substantially below the median blue-collar wage. It might be noted that when drivers were asked what they earned per hour, many believed they earned about $10.00 per hour.

Another comparison would be to calculate the hourly rate drivers would be earning if they were covered by the overtime provisions of the

Fair Labor Standards Act. With a work week of sixty hours, drivers would be paid forty hours at their normal rate and twenty hours at time and a half. Using this modification, the average hourly wage of $11.67 would amount to a normal rate of $10.03 for the typical driver. The modified union rate would be $12.58, the nonunion rate would be $9.21, and the hourly rate for owner-operators would be $10.31.[5]

CHAPTER 3

Hours of Work,
Hours of Rest

Unlike most employees, the pay and hours of truck drivers are not regulated by the minimum wage or the overtime provisions of the Fair Labor Standards Act (FLSA) administered by the U.S. Department of Labor.[1] Instead, truck driving is governed by the Hours of Service Regulations established by the U.S. Department of Transportation. Until January 2004, when the HOS Regulations were revised, these regulations required an eight-hour break after no more than ten hours of driving or fifteen hours of work including driving. Driving time was limited to sixty hours in seven days or seventy hours in eight days. The limit on drivers' weekly work time is, then, 150% of the forty-hour work week that typifies full-time employment in the United States.

Drivers are required to keep records of the time during which they are responsible for their equipment, their tractor and trailer. This time is divided between driving time, on-duty nondriving time, and rest breaks. On-duty nondriving time includes both time spent on work activities, such as loading and unloading, dropping and hooking, and tarping loads, and time spent waiting for a dispatch, to get into a dock, and for loading and unloading. Records of time are typically kept in a paper log.

As discussed in chapter 2, drivers are typically paid mileage rates or a percentage of revenue. Although these rates may implicitly include pay for on-duty nondriving work, time spent on such duties is seldom directly compensated. This provides an incentive for drivers to underreport such time in their logs to increase the hours available for compensated activities—that is, driving (for a more complete discussion of this issue, see the information on logbooks in chapter 7). Surveys of drivers' work time based on official logbooks undoubtedly undermeasure nondriving work time and consequently underreport actual work time of drivers.

To provide an accurate account of all the work done by drivers, the survey asked questions about the components of the drivers' work and rest time over four different time frames. First, the survey asked questions about the twenty-four hours immediately preceding the interview. These included inquiries on mileage, driving time, on-duty nondriving time, and sleep time. It was thought that the twenty-four hours preceding would be fresh in the drivers' minds and that therefore questions about this period would accurately capture drivers' utilization of time. Questions were then asked about the last completed trip. These covered similar issues—miles driven, driving time, and on-duty nondriving time —along with more specific questions on time spent on duties such as waiting for loading or unloading or dropping and hooking. Work time was also measured over the preceding seven days, with questions about days and hours worked, number of dispatches, and mileage. Finally, questions were asked about the pay for the last pay period and the total hours of driving and nondriving work in that pay period. Drivers were asked to provide answers based on their actual work rather than on their logbook reports.

Preceding Twenty-Four Hours

Work Time

Under the Hours of Service rules in place during this survey, drivers could legally work and drive sixteen hours in a twenty-four-hour period. For example, they might drive ten hours, rest eight hours, and then drive an additional six hours. They also could work sixteen hours in twenty-four if they worked fifteen hours, rested for eight hours and then worked an additional hour. How many hours do drivers typically work in a twenty-four-hour period?

■ Figure 17. Hours Worked in the Past Twenty-Four by Type of Employment

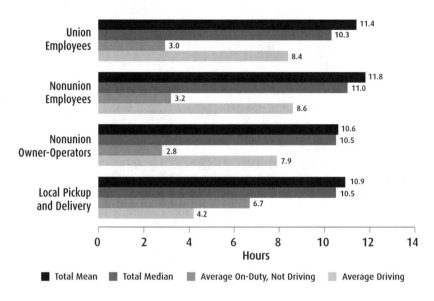

Total Mean   ■ Total Median   ■ Average On-Duty, Not Driving   ▨ Average Driving

Table 12 and figures 17–19 provide detailed information on time spent in driving and nondriving work in the twenty-four hours preceding our interviews. Figure 17 provides information on average hours spent working. Turning first to distinguishing those who had worked the previous day from those who had not, 6.5% of the overall sample had driven no miles in the preceding twenty-four hours. Distinguishing by type of employee, 10.0% of union employees, 5.1% of nonunion employees, and 7.9% of nonunion owner-operators reported not driving in the preceding twenty-four hours.

Of those who did drive, most worked in excess of eight hours. Nonunion owner-operators had the shortest average total hours, with 10.6 hours of work in the preceding twenty-four hours. Union employees ranked second, working 11.4 hours in the preceding twenty-four and nonunion employees reported the highest average hours, roughly 11.8 hours.[2] Median work hours were 10.5, 10.3, and 11.0, respectively.

Many drivers worked even longer hours. Twenty-five percent of

■ Table 12. Picture of the Last Twenty-Four Hours Working

| | ALL | EMPLOYEES | | OWNER-OPERATORS | LOCAL | OTR |
		UNION	NONUNION	(NONUNION)		
Observations	*520*	*43*	*340*	*135*	*59*	*461*
Miles Driven						
Mean	429.1	418.9	439.7	409.1	274.4	454.0
10th Percentile	125.0	250.0	100.0	100.0	80.0	150.0
25th Percentile	264.0	300.0	264.0	250.0	180.0	300.0
Median	400.0	365.0	420.0	400.0	250.0	450.0
75th Percentile	574.0	500.0	584.0	548.0	363.0	600.0
90th Percentile	700.0	653.0	800.0	700.0	460.0	784.0
Frequency No Miles	6.5%	10.0%	5.1%	7.9%	10.3%	5.9%
Hours Driven						
Mean	8.4	8.4	8.6	7.9	6.7	8.6
10th Percentile	3.5	5.5	3.0	3.0	2.5	3.5
25th Percentile	6.0	6.5	6.0	5.5	4.5	6.0
Median	8.0	8.0	8.0	8.0	7.0	8.5
75th Percentile	10.0	10.0	10.0	10.0	8.0	10.0
90th Percentile	14.0	12.0	14.0	12.0	11.0	14.0
Frequency No Hours	6.0%	10.0%	4.6%	7.3%	10.3%	5.4%
Hours On Duty Not Driving						
Mean	3.1	3.0	3.2	2.8	4.2	2.9
10th Percentile	0.3	0.5	0.3	0.3	1.0	0.3
25th Percentile	1.0	1.5	1.0	1.0	2.0	1.0
Median	2.0	2.0	2.0	2.0	3.5	2.0
75th Percentile	4.0	4.0	4.5	4.0	6.0	4.0
90th Percentile	7.0	5.0	8.0	6.0	8.0	6.5
Total Hours						
Mean	11.4	11.4	11.8	10.6	10.9	11.5
10th Percentile	5.8	6.5	6.5	5.0	7.5	5.5
25th Percentile	8.2	8.3	9.0	8.0	8.5	8.0
Median	11.0	10.3	11.0	10.5	10.5	11.0
75th Percentile	14.0	13.5	14.5	12.5	12.0	14.0
90th Percentile	18.0	20.0	18.3	16.5	16.0	18.0

drivers, those in or above the seventy-fifth percentile for total work time, had worked fourteen hours in the last twenty-four. Ten percent of drivers, those in or above the ninetieth percentile, reported working eighteen hours in the last twenty-four, two hours more than permitted by the Hours of Service Regulations. There is little difference in this pattern by type of driver, except that owner-operators work fewer hours at the seventy-fifth and ninetieth percentiles than do other drivers.

Driving Time

Average driving time for those who reported driving in the preceding twenty-four hours was 8.4 hours, median driving time was 8 hours. Figure 18 shows the distribution of hours of driving time by type of driver and work.[3] Nearly half (50.5%) had driven between seven and twelve hours in the preceding twenty-four hours. An additional 37.0% had driven less than seven hours. 7.1% had driven between thirteen and fifteen hours, and 5.4% reported driving at or beyond the limit on driving hours, sixteen or more hours.

Separating the data by type of driver, union employees had the shortest driving hours, with only 26.8% driving more than nine hours. Despite this, 6.6% reported driving at least sixteen hours in the last twenty-four. Nearly thirty-four percent (34.3%) of nonunion employees reported driving more than nine hours in the last twenty-four, and more than six percent(6.3%) reported driving sixteen or more hours in the same period. Somewhat over twenty-seven percent (27.2%) of owner-operators reported driving more than nine hours, but few (2.7%) reported driving more than sixteen hours. The distribution of hours for over-the-road drivers is similar to that for union and nonunion employees, but local drivers typically reported driving fewer hours, and none reported driving sixteen or more hours.

Nondriving Work Time

Table 12 illustrates that drivers typically spend 2 hours a day on nondriving work (median) but average 3.1 hours. The spread between the median and average suggests that, although drivers spend about 20% of

■ Figure 18. Hours Driving in the Previous Twenty-Four

All

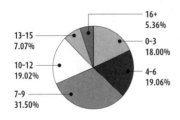

16+
5.36%

13–15
7.07%

0–3
18.00%

10–12
19.02%

4–6
19.06%

7–9
31.50%

Nonunion Owner-Operator

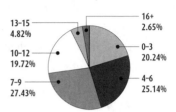

16+
2.65%

13–15
4.82%

0–3
20.24%

10–12
19.72%

4–6
25.14%

7–9
27.43%

Union Employees

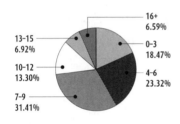

16+
6.59%

13–15
6.92%

0–3
18.47%

10–12
13.30%

4–6
23.32%

7–9
31.41%

Local

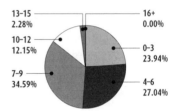

16+
0.00%

13–15
2.28%

10–12
12.15%

0–3
23.94%

7–9
34.59%

4–6
27.04%

Nonunion Employees

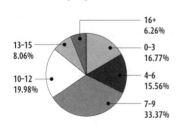

16+
6.26%

13–15
8.06%

0–3
16.77%

10–12
19.98%

4–6
15.56%

7–9
33.37%

Over-the-Road

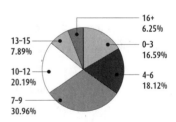

16+
6.25%

13–15
7.89%

0–3
16.59%

10–12
20.19%

4–6
18.12%

7–9
30.96%

their daily work time in nondriving work, many days require long periods of waiting and nondriving work. Figure 19 illustrates the distribution of hours of on-duty nondriving time in the last twenty-four hours. Only 14.2% of the full sample reported spending no time on other duties than driving; slightly under half (46.2%) of the sample reported spending one to two hours on other duties; 22.3% reported spending three to five hours on such duties. A smaller proportion of drivers reported spending longer periods on nondriving duties: 11.0% reported spending six to nine hours, 4.0% reported ten to fourteen hours, and 2.2% reported fifteen or more hours. A typical driver would then expect that every five or six days he or she would spend six or more hours, more than half of an average work day, in waiting, loading or other on-duty nondriving activities.

Nonunion employees spent more time on nondriving work than did union employees or owner-operators. Nearly twenty percent (20.3%) of nonunion employees spent at least six hours on nondriving work, only 13.5% of union drivers and 11.9% of owner-operators reported equivalent hours in the preceding twenty-four. Union employees were the most likely to spend no time on nondriving work (18.7%). Owner-operators were somewhat less likely to have zero hours of such work (16.7%), while nonunion employees were the least likely to avoid nondriving work time (12.6%). Local drivers spent more time on nondriving work than did over-the-road drivers. Few local drivers (7.0%) had no on-duty nondriving time, while 15.1% of over-the-road drivers spent no time in such work. Likewise, local drivers were less likely to have one to two hours of on-duty nondriving time (22.9% for local, compared to 48.7% for over-the-road.) Local drivers were more likely to spend three to five hours (35.4% compared to 20.9%), six to nine hours (23.8% compared to 9.5%), and ten or more hours (10.8% compared to 5.8%), on such duties than over-the-road drivers.[4] These results are consonant with the differences in the duties of local and over-the-road drivers.

■ Figure 19. Hours On-Duty, Not Driving in the Previous Twenty-Four

All

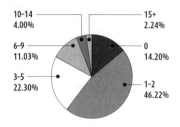

10–14 4.00%	15+ 2.24%
6–9 11.03%	0 14.20%
3–5 22.30%	1–2 46.22%

Nonunion Owner-Operator

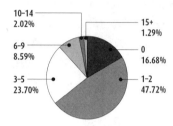

10–14 2.02%	15+ 1.29%
6–9 8.59%	0 16.68%
3–5 23.70%	1–2 47.72%

Union Employees

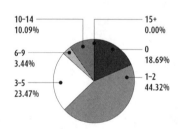

10–14 10.09%	15+ 0.00%
6–9 3.44%	0 18.69%
3–5 23.47%	1–2 44.32%

Local

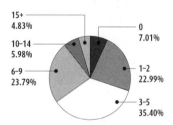

15+ 4.83%	0 7.01%
10–14 5.98%	1–2 22.99%
6–9 23.79%	3–5 35.40%

Nonunion Employees

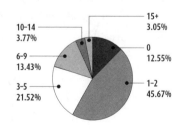

10–14 3.77%	15+ 3.05%
6–9 13.43%	0 12.55%
3–5 21.52%	1–2 45.67%

Over-the-Road

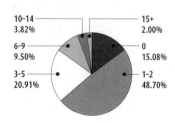

10–14 3.82%	15+ 2.00%
6–9 9.50%	0 15.08%
3–5 20.91%	1–2 48.70%

Sleep Time

Spurred by sensationalistic reports of drivers who sleep few hours as they drive the nation's highways, the adequacy of drivers' sleep time has become an issue of national concern. The long hours of work reported in this survey raise the concern that drivers may not be able to fit sufficient sleep into their arduous schedules.

Respondents were asked how many hours they had slept in the past twenty-four. Self-reported data on sleep has limitations. It tends to be answered in terms of when respondents went to bed rather than when they went to sleep. As with all questions about sensitive topics, there may be a tendency by respondents to answer in terms of what is acceptable rather than according to actual experience. There can also be overlap between nondriving work time and sleep time. Drivers may nap when they are on-duty but are not required to engage in effort, such as while waiting for loading or unloading. Such time will typically be recorded as off-duty time in logbooks but may be double counted in a few instances.

The survey data on hours of sleep is divided according to whether the interview was conducted face-to-face at a truck stop or over the phone. The phone interviews collected information on sleep in the last twenty-four hours the driver had worked. The sleep patterns reported in phone interviews are distinct from those obtained in the face-to-face interviews.

Beginning with in-person interviews (figure 20), the median driver reported sleeping eight hours in the last twenty-four (29.1%). An additional 44.6% reported sleeping more than eight hours, and 16.2% reported sleeping six to seven hours. A smaller group, 10.1% of the sample, reported five or fewer hours of sleep. Nearly eight percent (8.3%) reported sleeping between three and five hours; a small proportion (0.4%) reported one to two hours of sleep, and 1.4% of in-person interviewees reported not sleeping in the last twenty-four hours. This data suggests that the majority of drivers are getting reasonable amounts of sleep, but that slightly under 2% of drivers are sleeping very little in a twenty-four-hour period.

■ Figure 20. Sleep in the Past Twenty-Four Hours of a Workday

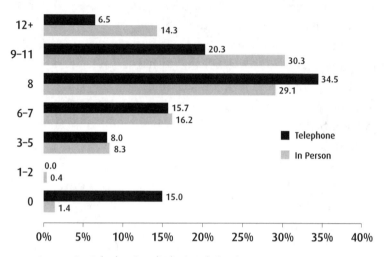

In person: Twenty-four hours immediately prior to the interview
Telephone: Most recent twenty-four hours worked (may be twenty-four hours prior to interview or
twenty-four hours worked prior to an extended break.)

The telephone interviews, which refer to the last twenty-four hours in which the respondent worked, indicate a similar pattern of sleep. Seventy-seven percent of drivers reported getting six or more hours of sleep. More telephone respondents reported sleeping eight hours (34.5%) than in-person respondents (29.1%), but fewer reported sleeping more than eight hours (26.8% compared to 44.6%). Similar percentages slept six or seven hours (15.7% compared to 16.2%, respectively).

The most notable difference is that 15% of the phone interviewees indicated that they had not slept in the last twenty-four hours they worked, while only 1.4% of in-person interviews reported no sleep in the past twenty-four hours. This difference between in-person and telephone interviews may have to do with the driver getting home after a long day and renewing acquaintances and doing long-delayed chores rather than sleeping. Yet this is not likely, as the phone interviews refer specifically to the *last twenty-four hours worked*. It appears that completing the final dispatch, returning to the domicile point, completing duties associated with finishing a trip, and then driving home do not allow the drivers time for needed rest.

Last Trip

A trip, defined as the activities beginning with a dispatch and continuing until the final load included in the dispatch is dropped, is a natural unit of measurement for drivers' work. A trip includes all of a driver's work duties and provides a comprehensive portrait of the drivers' work life. The questions asked about the drivers' last trip were particularly detailed and included information about origin and destination of the trip, product hauled, mileage, hours driven, and nondriving work broken down into working time and waiting time. Although most trips lasted one or more workdays, it was possible for a driver to make multiple trips in a single day.

Drivers averaged 707 miles on their last completed trip. The average trip required 13.4 hours of driving time, 2.3 hours of nondriving work time, and 5.7 hours of waiting time. The median trip was 500 miles, took 9.8 hours of driving time, 1.3 hours of nondriving work and 2 hours of waiting time.

Trip mileage varied greatly between drivers. The tenth percentile of drivers reported driving 150 miles, while those at the ninetieth percentile drove ten times as far, 1,500 miles. Union employees drove fewer miles per trip than did nonunion employees or nonunion owner-operators. The last trip of union employees averaged 431 miles, while nonunion owner-operators averaged 692 miles. The longest trips, which averaged 760 miles, were driven by nonunion employees. Median mileage shows less variation, but the pattern by type of driver remains —390 miles for union employees, 430 miles for nonunion owner-operators, and 560 miles for nonunion employees. Local drivers averaged 227 miles per trip, compared to the 789 miles averaged by over-the-road drivers.

Figure 26 provides information about hours of work on the last trip, dividing the time into driving time, waiting time (waiting for loading

■ Table 13. Picture of the Last Trip

	ALL	EMPLOYEES UNION	EMPLOYEES NONUNION	OWNER-OPERATORS (NONUNION)	LOCAL	OTR
Miles Driven						
Observations	566	49	364	150	67	499
Mean	706.8	431.2	759.6	692.0	226.9	788.9
10th Percentile	150.0	150.0	150.0	135.0	20.0	200.0
25th Percentile	300.0	200.0	310.0	250.0	95.0	370.0
Median	500.0	390.0	560.0	430.0	200.0	600.0
75th Percentile	900.0	528.0	1,000.0	862.0	334.0	1,000.0
90th Percentile	1,500.0	790.0	1,600.0	1,500.0	420.0	1,600.0
Hours Driven						
Observations	563	49	363	148	65	498
Mean	13.4	9.1	14.0	14.0	5.4	14.8
10th Percentile	3.0	3.0	4.0	2.5	1.0	4.0
25th Percentile	6.0	6.0	6.5	4.5	2.5	7.0
Median	9.8	8.5	10.0	8.8	5.0	10.0
75th Percentile	17.0	11.5	18.0	15.0	8.0	19.0
90th Percentile	26.0	16.0	30.0	27.0	10.0	30.0
Hours Waiting						
Observations*	468	35	299	131	47	421
Mean	5.7	3.0	5.4	7.6	1.6	6.3
10th Percentile	0.3	0.4	0.3	0.3	0.2	0.4
25th Percentile	0.9	0.5	0.8	1.3	0.5	1.0
Median	2.0	1.5	2.0	2.9	1.0	2.5
75th Percentile	5.0	3.0	5.0	7.0	2.0	5.5
90th Percentile	12.0	4.0	10.0	23.2	3.0	14.0
Frequency of none	15.8%	28.6%	16.5%	10.3%	24.2%	14.8%
Hours Working, Not Driving						
Observations*	484	43	315	124	60	424
Mean	2.3	3.2	2.2	2.2	1.7	2.5
10th Percentile	0.3	0.4	0.3	0.3	0.3	0.3
25th Percentile	0.5	0.8	0.5	0.5	0.5	0.5
Median	1.3	1.5	1.3	1.0	1.0	1.3
75th Percentile	3.0	3.3	3.0	2.6	2.0	3.3
90th Percentile	5.2	6.0	5.2	5.0	3.3	5.3
Frequency of none	13.9%	12.2%	12.3%	17.9%	6.3%	14.9%

*Statistics for hours waiting and hours working pertain to those with non-zero waiting and working time. The percentage of the sample with no time spent waiting or working is reported as frequency of none.

■ Figure 21. Hours Spent On-Duty Not Driving, Waiting, and Driving on the Last Trip by Type of Employment

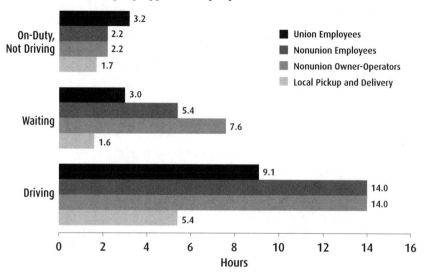

and unloading, and so on), and work time (dropping and hooking, loading or unloading actually done by the driver), where "work" is, in this context, used to denote physical work performed by the driver when he or she is not driving.

The trips of union employees took fewer hours than those of nonunion employees or owner-operators. Union employees averaged 15.3 hours on their last trip, compared to 21.6 hours for nonunion employees and 23.8 hours for owner-operators. Union drivers also had the lowest mean and median driving times, 9.1 and 8.5 hours, respectively, followed by owner-operators (14.0 and 8.8 hours, respectively), while nonunion employees had the longest trips, with a mean driving time of 14 hours and a median time of 10 hours. The spread between the median and mean again suggests that a small proportion of trips are very long. Among nonunion employees, those at the seventy-fifth percentile of trip driving time reported driving 18 hours on their last trip, while those at the ninetieth percentile reported driving 30 hours. The hours for nonunion owner-operators were 15 and 27, respectively.

Union employees reported shorter trips, 11.5 hours at the seventy-fifth percentile and 16 hours at the ninetieth percentile.

This pattern of results, with union employees reporting substantially shorter average trip lengths, but with greater similarity to nonunion drivers in median length and a similar pattern for driving hours, reflects differences in the type of work of these two types of drivers. Union employees are more likely to work for less-than-truck-load (LTL) companies and to work as local drivers than are nonunion drivers—10.5% of over-the-road drivers in our sample were union members, while 17.8% of local drivers reported being union members. Both types of drivers would be expected to have shorter trips. As a result, the mean trip mileage and driving time was substantially lower for union employees. Yet the similarity of the median mileage and hours suggests that the majority of nonunion employees also drive moderate-length trips. Long trips are more common among but do not dominate the work of nonunion employees.

It is claimed that nonunion employees and nonunion owner-operators wait more hours than union employees, and this was confirmed by the driver survey. At the median, waiting time for union employees was 1.5 hours, while nonunion employees waited 2.0 hours and nonunion owner-operators waited 2.9 hours. Mean waiting time was more divergent, at 3.0, 5.4, and 7.6 hours, respectively.

These figures, of themselves, do not demonstrate that nonunion employees are at a disadvantage with regard to waiting time. The longer waiting times may be the result of longer trips. To adjust for this we calculated the ratio of mean waiting time to mean driving time for our three groups. This ratio is 33% for union employees, 39% for nonunion employees, and 54% for nonunion owner-operators. Even allowing for the difference in trip lengths, it appears that nonunion employees and owner-operators have longer waiting times than union employees. The difference in the treatment in waiting time between union and nonunion employees—union employees are more likely to be compensated for waiting time than are nonunion employees—may account for some of this difference. The substantially longer waiting time of nonunion owner-operators, most of whom are single-truck operations, may be due to a lack of bargaining power over shippers and consignees.

Local pickup and delivery drivers had substantially lower waiting times than did over-the-road drivers, at 1.6 hours per trip for local drivers, against 6.3 for over-the-road. The ratio of waiting time to driving time is also lower, with waiting time being 29.6% of driving time for local drivers, and 42.6% of driving time for over-the-road drivers.

Time spent on nondriving work was somewhat higher for union drivers than for nonunion drivers or nonunion owner-operators, 3.2 hours on average for the former, 2.2 hours on average for the latter two groups. The medians are quite close, at 1.5, 1.3, and 1.0 hours, respectively. Nondriving work hours have a much less dispersed upper tail than do waiting time or driving time.

Last Seven Days

Miles Driven

Respondents drove an average of 2,126 miles in the seven days prior to the interview. This is close to the average mileage for nonunion employees (2,153 miles) and nonunion owner-operators (2,164 miles) but 276 miles higher than the average for union employees (1,850). Similarly, median mileage was 2,186 miles for all drivers, 2,200 for nonunion employees, 2,300 for nonunion owner-operators, and 2,000 for union employees. Local drivers drove 1,207 miles on average, as compared to 2,282 for over-the-road drivers.

Days Worked

The average driver worked five days out of the last seven calendar days, and the mean days of work were similar across groups of drivers (figure 27). However, nonunion employees and owner-operators had a more variable work week than did union employees. Fifty-five percent of union employees reported working five days in the last seven, as compared to 37% of nonunion employees and 34% of nonunion owner-operators. Forty-five percent of nonunion employees and 47% of owner-operators

■ Table 14. Picture of the Last Seven Days

	ALL	EMPLOYEES		OWNER-OPERATORS (NONUNION)	LOCAL	OTR
		UNION	NONUNION			
Observations	*566*	*49*	*367*	*148*	*67*	*499*
Miles Driven						
Mean	2,126	1,850	2,153	2,164	1,207	2,282
10th Percentile	700	60	600	1,000	0	1,000
25th Percentile	1,500	1,500	1,400	1,500	500	1,560
Median	2,186	2,000	2,200	2,300	1,000	2,300
75th Percentile	2,800	2,500	2,860	2,800	1,815	3,000
90th Percentile	3,500	3,000	3,600	3,500	2,500	3,600
Days Worked						
Mean	5.1	4.9	5.2	5.1	4.8	5.2
10th Percentile	3.0	4.0	3.0	3.0	3.0	3.0
25th Percentile	5.0	5.0	5.0	5.0	5.0	5.0
Median	5.0	5.0	5.0	5.0	5.0	5.0
75th Percentile	6.0	6.0	6.0	6.0	6.0	6.0
90th Percentile	7.0	6.0	7.0	6.0	6.0	7.0
Hours Worked						
Mean	63.2	59.8	66.4	56.9	62.4	66.2
10th Percentile	38.0	33.0	40.0	26.0	42.0	36.0
25th Percentile	50.0	50.0	50.0	40.0	46.5	50.0
Median	60.0	60.0	65.0	56.0	56.8	65.0
75th Percentile	75.0	70.0	80.0	70.0	70.0	80.0
90th Percentile	90.0	75.0	96.0	82.0	91.0	95.0
Number of Dispatches						
Mean	4.4	4.5	4.5	4.1	8.1	3.8
10th Percentile	1.0	1.0	1.0	1.0	0.0	1.0
25th Percentile	2.0	2.0	2.0	2.0	4.0	2.0
Median	4.0	4.0	4.0	3.0	5.0	3.0
75th Percentile	5.0	5.0	5.0	6.0	10.0	5.0
90th Percentile	8.0	8.0	8.0	8.0	16.0	7.0

■ Figure 22. Days Worked and Number of Dispatches in the the Previous Seven Days by Type of Employment

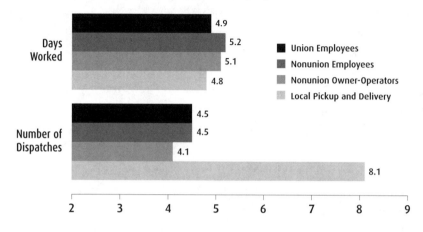

reported driving six to seven days in the past week, compared to 30% of union employees. Turning to short work weeks, 8% of union drivers reported working one day in the last seven, while 12% reported working four days. Ten percent of nonunion employees reported working four days, while 3% worked three days, 5% worked two days, 7% worked one day, and 2% did not work in the last seven days. Owner-operators showed a similar distribution of short work weeks. Local drivers were more likely to work a five-day week than were over-the-road drivers.

Hours of Work

Excluding those who reported no work in the previous week, drivers tended to work up to the legal limit. Drivers worked 60 hours in the last seven days at the median, and averaged 63.2 hours. Few drivers, only slightly more than 10% of the respondents, had worked 40 hours or less in the preceding seven days. A larger proportion had worked more than permitted by the Hours of Service Regulations: 25% of the respondents reported working at least 75 hours, and 10% reported working at least 90 hours.

Nonunion employees worked the longest hours, 65 hours at the median and 66.4 hours at the mean. Twenty-five percent reported working at least 80 hours in the previous seven days, and 10% reported working at least 96 hours. Union employees and nonunion owner-operators reported fewer hours of work and fewer worked extremely long hours. Union employees had worked an average of 59.8 hours in the preceding seven days. Among union employees, 25% reported working 70 or more hours, and 10% reported working 75 hours or more. Nonunion owner-operators worked an average of 56.9 hours. Among this group, 25% reported working at least 70 hours, and 10% reported working more then 82 hours in the preceding seven days.

These results suggest that the typical truck driver is working 60 hours per week and that a quarter of drivers are working more hours than are allowed by the Hours of Service Regulations. Some are working far more hours than are permitted by law. In combination with data on weeks of work collected in the survey, this suggests that drivers are working more than 3,000 hours per year, or 150% of the typical full-time work year. This pattern is most marked among nonunion employees, but is also prevalent among union employees and nonunion owner-operators.

Dispatches

Much like the data on hours worked in the last trip, the number of dispatches in the preceding seven days varied from driver to driver. From table 14 it is apparent that, consistent with the differences in their jobs, local drivers receive roughly twice as many dispatches as over-the-road drivers.

Union employees, nonunion employees, and owner-operators have a similar number of dispatches, ranging between 4.1 and 4.5. The distributions presented in figure 27 indicate that owner-operators have a lower mode (most common number of dispatches) than do union employees. This undoubtedly arises from owner-operators driving longer trips and therefore receiving fewer dispatches per week.

Last One-Week Pay Period

The last set of questions on working time covered the driver's last one-week pay period. Although most drivers were paid every seven days,

■ Table 15. Hours Worked in the Last One-Week Pay Period

	ALL	EMPLOYEES		OWNER-OPERATORS (NONUNION)	LOCAL	OTR
		UNION	NONUNION			
Observations	*543*	*49*	*349*	*143*	*66*	*477*
Hours Worked						
Mean	65.7	60.7	70.0	56.9	62.4	66.2
10th Percentile	38.0	42.0	42.0	24.0	42.0	36.0
25th Percentile	50.0	50.0	50.0	40.0	46.5	50.0
Median	62.0	60.0	65.0	56.0	56.8	65.0
75th Percentile	75.0	70.0	80.0	70.0	70.0	80.0
90th Percentile	95.0	80.0	100.0	82.0	91.0	95.0

some reported longer pay periods. The data reported in table 15 standardize these reports to a seven-day period for those who reported other periods. Hours worked in this case refers to hours spent on driving and nondriving work. As with all questions on working time, drivers were asked to report actual hours rather than those logged.

Based on pay periods, drivers averaged 65.7 hours in the prior seven-day pay period. This result was driven by the average 70.0 hours worked by nonunion employees. Union employees averaged 60.7 hours, and nonunion owner-operators averaged 56.9 hours. Median hours followed a similar pattern—high for nonunion employees, right on the 60-hour Hours of Service requirements for union employees, and somewhat lower for nonunion owner-operators. The slightly lower number of hours for nonunion owner-operators may reflect some tendency, apparently shared by many nonunion drivers, not to consider waiting time as work time.

Average and median times are close to or above sixty hours for each type of driver, which is comparable to our other data on working time. It again suggests that not only are drivers working far in excess of what is typically considered a full-time work week, but that a substantial proportion are regularly working more hours than are permitted by the Hours of Service Regulations.

Quality of Work Life

Drivers' work is demanding, with a typical work week of sixty hours or more. The nature of the work, picking up and delivering goods hundreds or thousands of miles from home, also places demands on drivers as it limits the frequency with which drivers return home and the time drivers have off between trips.

How often do drivers return home for at least a day—that is for twenty-four hours or more? An employee who worked a five-day week with weekends off would report, on average, 2.5 days since last staying at home for twenty-four hours (individual reports would vary between one and five days depending on the day of the week interviewed). In contrast, the median driver had been away from home for 4 days, and the average time away from home was 8.3 days (table 16). The most marked difference was between local drivers and over-the-road drivers. Local drivers, which can include those driving in a small region, reported being home an average 4.4 days previously, with a median of 2 days. Over-the-road drivers had a mean of 9 and a median of 4 days.

Conditions also differed between union employees, nonunion employees, and owner-operators.[5] The sharpest contrast was between owner-operators and union employees. Union employees reported last being home an average of 3.6 days previously, with a median of 2 days; owner-operators reported 10.6 days and 4 days, respectively. Nonunion employees fell between the two; the median time for returning home for twenty-four hours was four days, but their mean time away from home was 8.3 days.

The majority of drivers had been home for twenty-four hours in the last 1 to 5 days. Almost 79% of union employees, 58% of non-union employees, and 55% of owner-operators were in this category. Yet a substantial portion of drivers, particularly owner-operators and nonunion

■ Table 16. Quality of Work Life

	ALL	EMPLOYEES		OWNER-OPERATORS (NONUNION)	LOCAL	OTR
		UNION	NONUNION			
Last Time Home for Twenty-Four Hours *(in days)*						
Observations	*564*	*49*	*363*	*149*	*67*	*497*
Mean	8.3	3.6	8.3	10.6	4.4	9.0
10th Percentile	1.0	1.0	1.0	1.0	1.0	1.0
25th Percentile	2.0	1.0	2.0	2.0	1.0	2.0
Median	4.0	2.0	4.0	4.0	2.0	4.0
75th Percentile	7.0	5.0	8.0	14.0	5.0	10.0
90th Percentile	21.0	6.0	21.0	24.0	6.0	21.0
Hours Off before Last Trip						
Observations	*565*	*49*	*365*	*148*	*66*	*499*
Mean	24.6	23.3	25.5	23.0	15.0	26.2
10th Percentile	1.0	6.0	1.0	0.0	2.0	1.0
25th Percentile	8.0	9.0	8.0	7.0	9.0	8.0
Median	12.0	12.0	12.0	11.0	12.0	12.0
75th Percentile	28.0	24.0	30.0	24.0	15.0	36.0
90th Percentile	53.0	72.0	55.0	48.0	24.0	60.0

employees, were away from home for longer periods. More than twenty-five percent (25.5%) of nonunion employees and 31.1% of owner-operators had not been home for at least eight days, while 12.6% of nonunion employees and 18.7% of owner-operators had not been home for more than two weeks.

Considering the time between the last completed trip and the current trip, the median driver had 12 hours off; however, mean time off was 24.6 hours. There was little difference in mean or median time off between union and nonunion employees or owner-operators. Local drivers have fewer long breaks than over-the-road drivers. Mean time off was 15 hours for local drivers compared to 26.2 hours for over-the-road,

■ Table 17. Sleeping Arrangements

	LAST NIGHT	BETWEEN TRIPS
Bunk in Truck	70.1%	40.7%
In Truck, Not in Bunk	1.2%	1.1%
Home	23.5%	53.1%
Motel	4.3%	4.3%
Other	0.9%	0.8%

but median time for both was 12 hours. The difference in means reflected differences in the requirements of local and over-the-road work. Considering the length of over-the-road trips, the similarity in the median time off between trips suggests that over-the-road drivers typically have less time to rest than do local drivers.

Time off between trips does not correspond to time at home. The survey asked drivers both where they had slept the previous night and where they had slept between their previous and their current trip (table 17). The majority of drivers, 70.1% of respondents, reported that they had slept in the bunk in their truck on the previous night, while 23.5% reported sleeping at home, 4.3% reported sleeping in a motel, 1.2% reported sleeping in the truck but not in a bunk, and 0.9% reported sleeping elsewhere. Drivers were more likely to sleep at home between trips; 53.1% reported sleeping at home between their last and their current trip. Yet 40.7% of drivers reported sleeping in a bunk in their truck, 4.3% in a motel, 1.1% in the truck but not in the bunk, and 0.8% reported sleeping elsewhere. Apparently only slightly over half of the drivers were at home prior to the trip on which they were interviewed.

To summarize, our data indicates that, although most drivers have spent a day at home in the last week, a substantial proportion of drivers do not return home for extended periods. Over-the-road drivers' time off between trips is relatively short, given the length of trips and the amount of time spent away from home.

CHAPTER 4

Job Tenure and Stability

Managers of trucking firms and the trucking industry press have complained about a driver shortage for many years. Trucking firms have been compelled to engage in extensive recruiting and have offered wage increases, signing bonuses, and improved equipment to attract drivers. Yet what appears to be a driver shortage to the firm may be partly a problem with driver turnover. Firms with high turnover will have problems with recruiting even in industries where there is no shortage of employees. They may also be forced to engage in training if the employees they are hiring are from the less experienced or less qualified segment of the industry labor force.

The driver survey asked about drivers' work experience and background and specifically about the length of time they had worked as a truck driver (occupational experience), the length of time they had been with their current firm (service with current employer), and whether the driver had quit a driving job in the last twelve months. From this data it appears that drivers remain in their occupation but do not remain with the same employer for very long, particularly when compared to other blue-collar workers. Drivers are also more likely to quit a job than other blue-collar workers. This high rate of turnover contributes to the hiring problems faced by trucking firms.

Occupational Experience and Service with the Current Employer

Occupational Experience

Truck driving is a career occupation for the majority of drivers. Seventy-nine percent of those interviewed had worked as a driver for five years or more, and 40% had been a driver for at least fifteen years. Union drivers have more experience than nonunion drivers. Nearly eighty-eight percent (87.6%) of union employees reported driving five or more years, and 62.1% had been employed as drivers for more than fifteen years. These figures are 74.0% and 32.9%, respectively, for nonunion drivers.

Owner-operators were almost as likely as union employees to have five or more years of experience (87.3%), but a lower proportion (48.6%) had more than fifteen years of experience as a driver. The large proportion of owner-operators with long occupational tenure reflects a career path in which owner-operators start as employee drivers before owning their own truck.

Service with the Current Employer

Although most drivers had been driving commercial trucks for many years, few had been with their current employer for very long.[1] Only 24.4% of drivers reported working for their current firm for four or more years. In contrast, 34.1% of all drivers reported being employed for their current firm for ten months or less, 45.1% had worked for their current firm for fifteen months or less, and half had been with their employer for eighteen months or less.

Union employees had the longest service with their current employer: 45.3% of union employees had been with their current employer for at least four years while only 20.9% of nonunion employees had been with their current employer that long. At the other end of the spectrum, 38.6% of nonunion employees had worked for their current employer for ten months or less, while only 6.7% of union employees reported working for their current employer for such a brief period.

Table 18. Occupation and Employer Tenure

| | ALL DRIVERS | EMPLOYEES | | OWNER-OPERATORS |
		UNION	NONUNION	(NONUNION)
Occupational Tenure*				
1 Year	8.9%	9.9%	11.2%	3.0%
2 Years	3.7%	0.0%	4.2%	4.2%
3–4 Years	8.4%	2.5%	10.7%	5.4%
5–7 Years	11.3%	6.2%	12.1%	10.7%
8–10 Years	12.9%	5.8%	14.7%	11.0%
11–15 Years	14.8%	13.5%	14.3%	17.0%
More than 15 Years	40.0%	62.1%	32.9%	48.6%
Tenure with Employer				
1 Month	5.6%	0.7%	6.5%	
2 Months	2.8%	0.0%	3.3%	
3–4 Months	6.7%	0.0%	7.9%	
5–7 Months	11.6%	0.0%	13.2%	
8–10 Months	7.4%	6.0%	7.7%	
11–15 Months	11.0%	13.5%	10.6%	
16–24 Months	13.9%	13.3%	13.8%	
25–33 Months	2.0%	0.0%	2.4%	
34–40 Months	6.6%	5.9%	6.8%	
41–48 Months	7.9%	12.0%	7.2%	
More than 48 Months	24.4%	45.3%	20.9%	
Quit Rates				
Respondents who have quit a driving job in the last 12 months	24.2%	10.1%	26.2%	25.4%

Note: All statistics are calculated with weights proportional to probability of appearing in the sample.
*The number of years reported by the respondent.

■ Figure 23. Union Tenure Compared to Nonunion Tenure

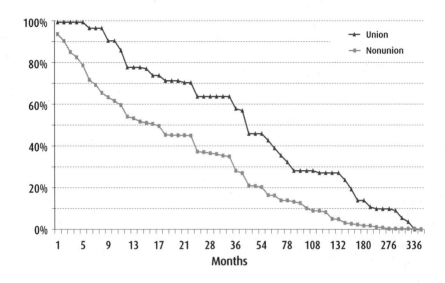

The difference between union and nonunion employees may reflect nonunion employees moving between jobs in search of better pay. Union members have less reason to move, as rates have been standardized by bargaining and there is little gain from moving between firms.

Quit Rates

Quit rates provide another measure of job attachment and turnover. Respondents were asked about voluntary quits but not about layoffs and involuntary terminations. Nearly twenty-four percent (24.2%) of all drivers reported having quit a driving job in the preceding twelve months. Again, this figure differs sharply by union membership and employment status. Among union employees, 10.1% reported quitting a driving job in the last twelve months, while 26.2% of nonunion employees and 25.4% of owner-operators had terminated a lease in the last year.

Table 19. Employer Tenure of Drivers and Blue-Collar Workers

| YEARS OF SERVICE | BLUE-COLLAR (CPS) | ALL DRIVERS | EMPLOYEES | | TYPE OF WORK | |
			UNION	NONUNION	LOCAL	OTR
Less than 1	21.7%	36.5%	14.3%	40.5%	35.9%	36.9%
1	8.8%	15.0%	15.5%	14.7%	8.8%	16.3%
2	10.5%	9.5%	6.6%	10.0%	0.8%	11.2%
3	10.5%	7.8%	6.8%	7.9%	12.3%	6.9%
4	6.8%	7.4%	11.1%	6.7%	5.8%	7.7%
5	5.9%	4.4%	6.9%	4.0%	5.4%	4.3%
6–10	15.8%	11.3%	11.8%	11.2%	20.2%	9.5%
11–15	7.5%	4.8%	13.3%	3.3%	7.2%	4.3%
16–20	4.8%	1.2%	4.0%	0.7%	2.9%	0.8%
21–25	3.5%	0.8%	0.9%	0.8%	0.8%	0.2%
26 or more	3.5%	1.5%	8.9%	0.2%	0.0%	1.8%

Truck Drivers' Employer Service Compared to a National Blue-Collar Sample

The April 1993 Benefits Supplement to the Current Population Survey (CPS), a special suppliment of the monthly labor force survey conducted by the Census Bureau, includes a question on years of service with the current employer. Since this survey tabulated answers in years rather than by months, we converted our data on drivers to years. We limited the sample to blue-collar males to improve the comparability of the national data.

Service with the current employer is considerably shorter among truck drivers than among typical blue-collar males. More than a third of all drivers reported less than one year with their current employer, but only 21.7% of the CPS sample falls into this category. Drivers were also more likely to have more than one but less than two years with their current employer than the CPS sample, with 15.0% and 8.8%, respec-

■ Figure 24. Driver Tenure Compared to Blue-Collar Tenure

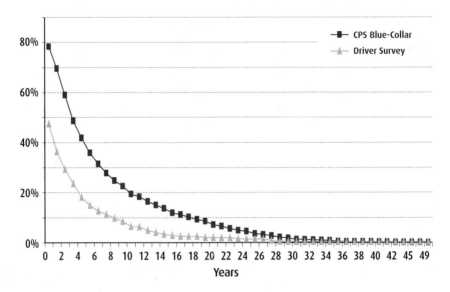

tively, in this category. The proportion of blue-collar males is almost always larger than the proportion of drivers in each category once service of two or more years is considered. For example, 10.5% of the CPS sample have at least two but less than three years with their current employer, while only 7.8% of the driver workforce falls in this category. The differences become more marked with increased years of service. While very few drivers report sixteen or more years with their current employer, 11.8% of blue-collar males do.

In summary, the driver workforce changes employers often. Although some drivers and some segments of the industry show strong employer attachment, the majority have much less attachment than is typical of the blue-collar labor force. Such rapid turnover may impose costs on employers, as they are forced to continually recruit and train employees. This suggests that what appears to the firms to be a shortage of drivers is in part a very high turnover rate.

CHAPTER 5

Owner-Operators in the Driver Labor Force

Owner-Operators are an important component of the driver workforce. Owner-operators have more control over their work than do other drivers. Typically they are able to decide which loads to accept and have more command over their time. This control comes at the cost of greater risk. Owner-operators own or lease trucks and typically pay both the capital and operating costs of the truck.

Many of the questions asked of owner-operators, such as those about pay systems, allocation of time, and benefits, paralleled those asked of employee drivers. Other questions, such as those on the number of trucks owned, truck financing, sources of loads and sources of payment, days to payment, and distinctions between gross and net revenue, were specific to owner-operators. One hundred and fifty-three owner-operators, 25.6% of the sample, were interviewed in the first wave of the driver survey.

Who Becomes an Owner-Operator? How Much Do They Own?

Years as Owner-Operator

Although some owner-operators have worked for themselves for many years, most have been owner-operators for 4 years or less. Median tenure as an owner-operator is 3 years, but mean tenure is 7.9 years. The spread between the median and mean reflects the bifurcation between

■ Table 20. Years as Owner-Operator

	ALL	OTR	LOCAL*
Mean	7.9	7.9	6.8
10th Percentile	1	1	1
25th Percentile	1	1	1
Median	3	4	2
75th Percentile	13	13	11
90th Percentile	20	20	16

*Eleven observations in sample.

a large group of drivers who have been owner-operators for many years and another large group who have only recently become owner-operators. Twenty-five percent of the sample reported working as owner-operators for 13 years or more, while 10% reported having been owner-operators for 20 or more years. At the other end of the scale, 25% of respondents reported having been owner-operators for 1 year or less.

Relatively few owner-operators worked as local drivers. Only eleven respondents reported being both owner-operators and local drivers.

■ Figure 25. Number of Trucks Owned

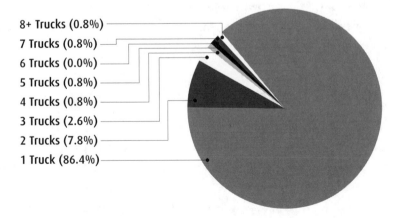

8+ Trucks (0.8%)
7 Trucks (0.8%)
6 Trucks (0.0%)
5 Trucks (0.8%)
4 Trucks (0.8%)
3 Trucks (2.6%)
2 Trucks (7.8%)
1 Truck (86.4%)

Removing local owner-operators from the sample increased the median years as an owner-operator to four years, but did not alter the average years as an owner-operator.

Number of Trucks
The typical owner-operator owns a single truck. Few own more than two trucks. Nearly eight-six percent (86.4%) of the owner-operators reported owning a single truck, and an additional 7.8% reported owning two trucks, while 2.6% owned three trucks and 3.2% reported owning more than three trucks. One respondent reported owning seventy-five trucks.

Owning and Leasing
Owner-operators may either own their trucks or obtain a lease on the truck. Leasing is relatively uncommon: 14.1% of owner-operators with one truck lease their truck, while 5.9% of those with two or more trucks lease both trucks. In contrast, 85.9% of owner-operators with one truck own the truck, and 88.0% of those with two or more trucks own their trucks. Nearly six percent (6.1%) of those with more than one truck both own and lease trucks.

Financing of Trucks
The majority of owner-operators, 58.2%, finance their trucks through banks. Approximately equal proportions self-finance (13.3%), finance through the firm that holds their lease (12.8%), or finance through the truck dealer (12.0%). Smaller numbers finance through the manufacturer (3.0%) or obtained their truck as a gift or inheritance (0.7%).

■ Table 21. Ownership of Trucks

	ONE TRUCK	TWO OR MORE TRUCKS
Own Truck	85.9%	88.0%
Lease Truck	14.1%	5.9%
Both	n.a.	6.1%

■ Figure 26. Financing of Trucks by Owner-Operators

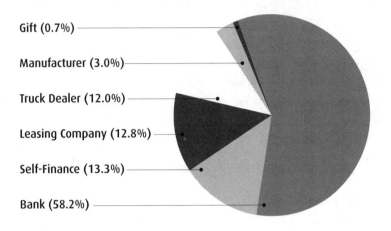

Gift (0.7%)

Manufacturer (3.0%)

Truck Dealer (12.0%)

Leasing Company (12.8%)

Self-Finance (13.3%)

Bank (58.2%)

Sources of Shipments and Payments

Most owner-operators (73.3%) obtain their loads through a permanent lease. The next largest source of shipments is brokers (17.3%), while contracts with shippers account for 6.8% of shipments. A small proportion of the sample (2.6%) reported obtaining shipments themselves or that the company they worked for brokered their own freight. All but 10% of the respondents reported receiving their payment from the company to whom they were leased, while 5.1% reported being paid by brokers and 4.1% were paid by shippers.

■ Table 22. Owner-Operators' Sources of Shipments and Payments

	SHIPMENTS	PAYMENTS
Permanent Lease	73.3%	90.4%*
Brokers	17.3%	5.1%
Contract with Shippers	6.8%	4.1%
Other	2.6%	0.4%

*Includes short-term relationship established by broker.

The relatively high proportion of owner-operators working under permanent leases suggests that owner-operators serve as an alternative to a conventional employment relationship. Rather than hiring employees, firms contract with owner-operators to obtain the freight capacity they require. The relationship between owner-operators and their leasers is no more permanent than that with employees. The survey finds that 44% of owner-operators have been with their leaser for one year or less, an additional 13% have been with the leaser for one to two years, and 12% have been with the leaser for two to three years.

Days to Payment

Owner-operators assume considerable risk for operating expenses and have legitimate concerns about delays in payments. Respondents to the driver survey indicated that 19.2% were paid within four days of completing a trip, and an additional 7.8% were paid within five to six days of completing a trip. Most drivers, 35.9%, were paid seven days after the trip, and an additional 23.1% were paid within two weeks. Very few owner-operators, 14.2% of our respondents, reported having to wait more than two weeks to be paid.

■ Figure 27. Owner-Operators' Days to Payment

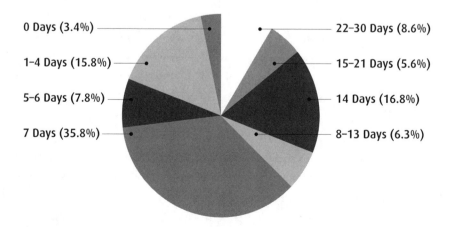

0 Days (3.4%)

1-4 Days (15.8%)

5-6 Days (7.8%)

7 Days (35.8%)

22-30 Days (8.6%)

15-21 Days (5.6%)

14 Days (16.8%)

8-13 Days (6.3%)

■ Table 23. Reasons for Becoming an Owner-Operator

	NOT AT ALL IMPORTANT		→	VERY IMPORTANT	
	1	2	3	4	5
Wanted to Be Independent	4.7%	2.4%	13.1%	16.0%	63.7%
Wanted to Make More Money	2.1%	5.6%	14.8%	20.0%	57.5%
Felt it Was the Only Way to Get a Job in the Industry	67.9%	10.0%	11.0%	1.6%	9.4%
Wanted to Have More Flexible Hours and Better Working Conditions	16.3%	4.8%	12.7%	20.6%	45.6%
Wanted to Grow a Business	11.4%	7.8%	17.5%	11.3%	51.8%

Other Reasons for Becoming an Owner-Operator

Personal Decision	62.4%
Being Able to Select Truck	9.9%
Terminated from Previous Job	6.2%
More Time at Home	3.5%
Personal Reasons Such as Having Wife on Trip	3.2%
Inherited the Business	2.7%
Bored or Wanted to See Country	2.5%

Willingness to Take More Work at the Current Rate

One measure of whether owner-operators are satisfied with their situation is whether they would accept additional work at their current rate. Those who answer affirmatively are likely satisfied with their current rate and believe they could earn more by taking on additional work. Those who do not may either already have as much freight as they can handle or be dissatisfied with current rates. The respondents to our survey were almost evenly split, half reporting they would take more work at the current rate, half saying they would not. This suggests that a substantial proportion, amounting to half or more, of the owner-operators are satisfied with the rates they are currently being paid.

■ Figure 28. Reasons for Becoming an Owner-Operator

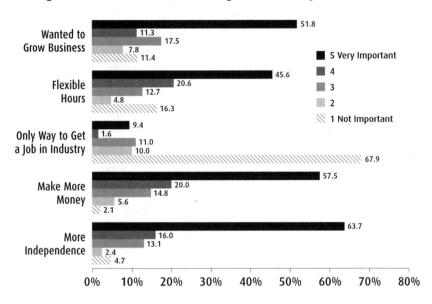

Reasons for Becoming an Owner-Operator

Self-employment may be a means of improving one's economic condition and gaining additional control over one's work life. The driver survey asked a series of questions about why owner-operators decided to become self-employed. Owner-operators were presented with a series of reasons for becoming an owner-operator and asked to rank the importance of the reasons to their decision. The most important reasons were a desire to be independent and to make additional money. Nearly sixty-four percent (63.7%) of drivers said that wanting to be independent was very important to their decision, and 57.5% stated that making more money was very important to their decision. Wanting to grow a business (51.8%) and having more flexible hours (45.6%) were somewhat less important. Becoming an owner-operator has been a means of obtaining a job in the motor freight industry in the past; it is less important currently because of the driver shortage. Nonetheless, 9.4% of respondents reported they believed that becoming an owner-operator was the only way to get a job in the industry.

Thirty percent of the drivers cited additional reasons for becoming an owner-operator. The majority of these cited personal reasons such as working as an owner-operator being an individual goal. Contrary to conventional beliefs about drivers, few decided to become owner-operators to be able to select the truck they drove. Only 9.9% of those who cited other reasons, or 3% of owner-operators, cited this as a reason for becoming an owner-operator.

Data from other parts of the driver survey can illuminate some of the reasons for becoming an owner-operator. Making more money was an important reason why drivers became owner-operators, but data on annual earnings suggest that relatively few owner-operators actually do better than their employee counterparts. Although this does not suggest that owner-operators may be more satisfied with their work for non-monetary reasons, it does appear that the belief that becoming an owner-operator will result in higher earnings is, for most drivers, illusory.

CHAPTER 6

The Utilization and Effects of New Technologies

Modern communications and computing technologies are becoming an integral part of the economy. This trend is also true in trucking. Computers, and the accompanying software, provide efficient dispatching, determine routing, and schedule maintenance. Until recently, however, advanced technologies have remained at corporate headquarters or at terminals, and although these technologies have affected the drivers' job, the drivers themselves have not used the technologies.

This has changed in the last decade. As computers have become smaller and more rugged, and as wireless communications technologies have become more ubiquitous, these technologies have begun to move onto the trucks, and drivers have begun to use the new technologies directly. Cellular phones and two-way radios provide direct communication between drivers, their firms, and customers without the driver having to stop; auto locators provide firms with information about the current location of the truck; and satellite systems serve both functions. Technologies such as barcode readers provide more accurate tracking of freight. Mobile computers such as laptops can aid owner-operators in evaluating cargoes they are offered, while e-mail and Internet communications permit them to search for loads and rapidly communicate in writing with brokers, leasers, and potential customers.

Although these technologies have the potential to improve the efficiency of both operations and the drivers' work, this depends both on the spread of the technologies and on how they are used. Availability does not put the technologies on the truck, and once on the truck, the technologies may not be used in an effective fashion.

This chapter explores the availability of advanced technologies on trucks and their effect on efficiency and the work of drivers. The first set of figures present data on the availability and use of technologies on trucks, the second considers drivers' views of these technologies, and the third reviews several measures of efficiency. The last set of charts illustrates the effect of onboard satellite systems, the most advanced truckboard technology, on efficient use of the truck and on the working conditions of drivers.

The analysis provided in this chapter finds that some technologies, such as satellite systems, are spreading very rapidly, while others, such as laptop computers, mobile faxes, and e-mail, are uncommon. In contrast with their effect on communication, technologies have yet to influence routing. Drivers are generally satisfied with the new technologies, and dissatisfaction is most typically associated with costs or with

■ Figure 29. Use of Technologies in Trucks

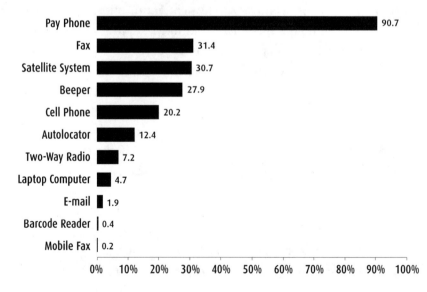

■ Table 24. Use of Technologies in Trucks

TECHNOLOGY (GADGET)	PERCENTAGE USING GADGET	RANK OF GADGET	HIGHEST RANKED GADGET	NUMBER OF USES IN 24 HOURS (MEDIAN)
Pay Phone	90.7%	1	7.9%	
Fax	31.4%	2	8.0%	3
Satellite System	30.7%	10	37.3%	4
Beeper	27.9%	3	18.0%	0
Cell Phone	20.2%	6	30.0%	2
Autolocator	12.4%	9	1.0%	0**
Two-Way Radio	7.2%	4	3.2%	1
Laptop Computer	4.7%	7	1.4%	0
E-mail	1.9%	11	0.6%	1
Barcode Reader	0.4%	8	0.3%	2
Mobile Fax	0.2%	12	0.3%	—

Gadgets are ranked from the least technologically sophisticated (1) to most technologically sophisticated (12). The column for highest ranked gadget reports the percentage of drivers for whom a particular gadget was the most technologically sophisticated. For example, a two-way radio was the most technologically sophisticated gadget used by 3.2% of drivers.

*Individuals may not be aware whether autolocator is operating.
**Number of observations is too small for accurate estimates.

limitations of the technology such as restricted range or missing features. A closer look at satellite systems indicates that these systems are associated with greater mileage; those with these systems report driving an additional fifteen thousand miles annually. Yet there is little evidence that satellites are associated with improvements in other aspects of efficiency or improve the income or work life of drivers.

Technologies Used or on the Truck

Respondents were asked a series of questions about the presence of various technologies (gadgets), their use of the gadgets, and their views on the most advanced gadget on their truck. In addition, the survey asked about the use of various technologies for routing.

All gadgets were assigned a rank reflecting their technological sophistication. These ranks are reported in table 24. Respondents were first asked whether they had the gadget on their truck or used the gadget. They were then asked the number of times they had used their most sophisticated (highest-ranked) gadget to contact their dispatcher in the last twenty-four hours. Respondents were also asked what they liked and disliked about their gadget.

Similar questions were asked about technologies used for routing. Here the topic of interest is the degree to which new technologies are supplanting the road atlas and CB as sources of routing information.

Respondents were asked whether they used the routing aid, how many times they had used it in the last twenty-four hours, and, for the more advanced aids, how long they had been using that aid.

Use of Technology

Use of communications technologies is increasing rapidly, but other technologies have made limited progress onto trucks (figure 29). The most ubiquitous technology remains the pay phone. Nearly ninety-one percent (90.7%) of drivers reported using a pay phone in the last twenty-four hours. The other common technologies are communications technologies: faxes (31.4%), satellite systems (30.7%), beepers (27.9%), and cellular phones (20.2%). Satellite systems are a new, sophisticated, and expensive technology. Their widespread use may reflect the prominence of the automotive industry, with its requirement of timely information on freight in the Midwest. In contrast, some of the technologies that have been more widely reported upon in the press, such as E-mail (1.9% reported using) and laptop computers (4.7%), are less likely to be on the truck or to be used. The relative rarity of barcode readers, used by only 0.4% of the sample, may reflect the relatively small number of local drivers in the sample.

Figure 30 and the last column of table 24 report the median number of times various technologies had been used in the past twenty-four

■ Figure 30. Use of Technologies in Past Twenty-Four Hours

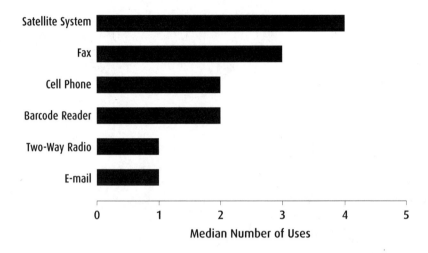

hours. Satellite systems were used most frequently: median usage was four times per day. The relative frequency of their use may reflect the convenience of the system and the fact that the driver is not responsible for the cost of the call. Faxes were the second-most commonly used system: median usage was three times per day. Cellular phones and barcode readers were used twice a day, while e-mail and two-way radios were typically used only once per day. The median use of several devices, beepers, laptop computers, autolocators, and mobile faxes, was zero. For mobile faxes, this likely reflects the small number found in the survey. Limited use of laptops may reflect their role as a tool used between rather than during trips. The low utilization of beepers, a technology that is ubiquitous, may reflect the limitations of the device over long distances.

There are new routing technologies, such as map CDs and Internet mapping, that provide up-to-date information and might improve drivers' ability to choose routes for their trips. The driver survey does not indicate that such technologies are in fact being adopted. Turning to routing, we find that road atlases, CBs, and the dispatcher are the main routing aids. Among the newer technologies, 13.4% of drivers reported

■ Table 25. Use of Technologies for Routing

ROUTING AID	PERCENTAGE USING ROUTING AID	NUMBER OF USES IN LAST 24 HOURS (MEDIAN)	MEDIAN NUMBER OF MONTHS SINCE BEGAN USING ROUTING AID
Paper Atlas	94.0%	1	n.a.
CB for Routing	64.1%	0	n.a.
Dispatcher	33.6%	0	n.a.
Cell Phone	13.4%	0	6
Onboard Computer	8.8%	2	6
PC/Internet	3.9%	0	5

using cell phones for routing, 8.8% reported using an onboard computer, and 3.9% reported using the Internet. Responses to the question, "When did you first start using this device?" suggest that the low penetration of new technologies may reflect their relative newness—the typical driver using a cell phone, an onboard computer, or PC/Internet for routing had been using the technology for less than half a year.

Drivers' Views of Technologies

Drivers have a positive view of the technologies on their trucks. As noted, each technology was ranked and drivers were asked what they liked and disliked about the highest-ranked technology they used.

Most drivers liked their technologies because, in various ways, they made communication with others easier and saved time. Almost 27% of drivers liked their device because it allowed "people" to get in touch. An additional 14.8% indicated that it improved communication with their family. A similar percentage (14.3%) indicated that their gadget improved communication with their firm, either by allowing them to get information from their firm (8.9%) or by easing communication with their dispatcher (5.3%). The devices also helped drivers obtain aid when a breakdown occurred; 8.9% of drivers reported their device was

■ Figure 31. What Drivers Like about the Technologies They Use

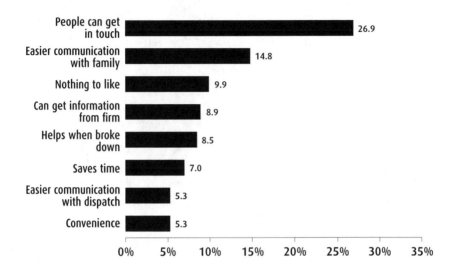

■ Figure 32. What Drivers Dislike about the Technologies They Use

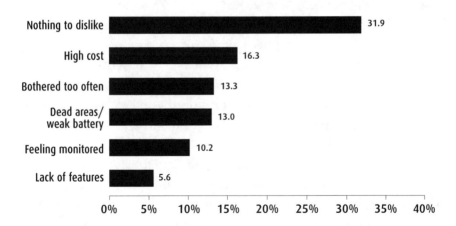

useful in such instances. Only 9.9% of drivers reported that there was nothing to like about their device.

Few drivers expressed strong dislikes about the devices they used, and, when they did, the dislikes had to do with costs or technical deficiencies of the device. Almost 32% of respondents stated there was nothing to dislike about their device. Sixteen percent (16.3%) found that the device cost too much, 13.0% reported technical problems such as dead areas or weak batteries, and 5.6% reported that their device lacked important features. There was also evidence that the devices were perceived as making communication too easy. Thirteen percent (13.3%) of drivers reported that their device made it too easy to reach them, and 10.2% reported that it made them feel monitored.

Measures of Efficiency

Efficient operations are important to the motor freight industry as well as to shippers and receivers. They are also important to drivers, as improvements in efficiency may be used to improve their earnings and working conditions.

Most of the measures of efficiency used to assess the industry, such as operating ratios, revenue per pound, and revenue per mile, are not available from driver interviews. The interviews nevertheless yielded several types of data related to efficiency on the last trip: miles driven with an empty trailer, whether the load on the trailer was limited by weight or volume, and the average speed of the trip. The first measure, empty or deadhead miles, reflects the number of nonrevenue miles on a trip. The second measures efficiency of loading; trucks that are limited by weight or volume are full and therefore represent an efficient load. The survey also allows us to calculate two measures of speed on the last trip. The first is the ratio of trip mileage to the driver's report of the time the trip took (miles per reported hour). The second is the ratio of trip mileage to the elapsed trip time, the time that elapsed from the time the driver was dispatched until he or she dropped the load. Additional measures of efficiency could be developed by considering amount of time spent waiting on each trip, but this data has been discussed in other chapters.

The data on efficiency is presented for all drivers and is then broken down according to whether the driver was an over-the-road employee, an over-the-road owner-operator, or a local driver (either employee or owner-operator).

Empty Miles

Empty miles, miles driven with an empty trailer, are unevenly distributed. The average trip includes 73.1 empty miles, but the median trip has no empty miles. Most of the empty miles occur on relatively few trips. The seventy-fifth percentile of the sample drove 90 empty miles on their last completed trip, while the ninetieth percentile drove 240 empty miles. The distribution of empty miles is similar for over-the-road employees and owner-operators, though employees drive somewhat more empty miles than owner-operators, on average (78 vs. 67 miles). Empty miles are more common among local pickup and delivery drivers, but these drivers typically drive fewer empty miles. The average local driver had 54.5 empty miles per trip, and the median local driver had 10 empty miles. The local driver at the seventy-fifth percentile drove 90 miles with an empty truck, the exact number driven by the seventy-fifth percentile driver for the overall sample. Yet at the ninetieth percentile the local driver had only 150 empty miles, versus 240 empty miles for the overall sample.

Loading on the Current Trip

Trucks operate under various load restrictions, two of the most important being the limits on weight and volume. The weight of loads and the maximum volume of trailers are limited by state and federal regulations.[1] If trucks are loaded efficiently, they should be at or close to the weight or volume capacity of their truck.[2] The driver survey asked two questions about the loading on the current trip: "Could you have loaded more if you were not limited by the weight of the load?" and "Could you have loaded more if you were not limited by the volume of the load?"

■ Table 26. Miles with Empty Trailer

| | ALL DRIVERS | OTR | | LOCAL |
		EMPLOYEES	OWNER-OPERATORS	
Mean	73.1	78.0	67.0	54.5
10th Percentile	0	0	0	0
25th Percentile	0	0	0	0
Median	0	0	0	10
75th Percentile	90	90	80	90
90th Percentile	240	270	248	150

The responses to these questions can be divided into four categories: loads limited by weight, loads limited by volume, loads limited by weight and volume, and loads not limited by either.

Turning to the last category, 38.4% of all respondents reported that their loads were not limited by either weight or volume. This varied by type of driver and work. Over-the-road employee drivers were the most likely to report their load was not limited (41.5%). Local drivers ranked second, with 37.3% reporting no limits, and owner-operators were the least likely to have loads that were unrestricted by weight or volume (31.7%).

Turning to the ways in which loads were restricted, volume restrictions are more common than weight restrictions. In all, 10.2% of loads were restricted by weight, 18.4% were limited by volume, and 33.0% of

■ Table 27. Load Limited by Weight or Volume

| | ALL DRIVERS | OTR | | LOCAL |
		EMPLOYEES	OWNER-OPERATORS	
Limited by Weight	10.2%	7.8%	13.5%	15.6%
Limited by Volume	18.4%	17.5%	21.3%	17.9%
Limited by Both	33.0%	33.3%	33.5%	29.2%
Limited by Neither	38.4%	41.5%	31.7%	37.3%

loads were limited by both weight and volume. This pattern is consistent across our groupings of drivers, and given sample size, there is little difference evident in the pattern of restriction across these groups.

The data on length of and time spent on a trip can be combined to calculate a driver's speed during the trip. The average speed when driving is calculated as the ratio of trip length to reported driving time. The typical speed is somewhat over 50 miles per hour: the average is 54.6 mph for employee drivers and 51.4 mph for owner-operators, the medians are modestly lower than the averages. Local drivers, who are more likely to be driving in metropolitan areas and make more stops per trip, average 40.9 mph with a median of 44.0 mph.

Speed while driving does not necessarily correspond to the overall speed of the trip as the latter is affected not only by driving time but also by time spent on other duties and by rest time. Accounting for time other than driving time results in a halving of truck speed for over-the-road drivers. Employees who are driving over-the-road average 27.4 mph while over-the-road drivers who are owner-operators average 23.4 mph. Median speeds are somewhat less than average speeds. Trips by local drivers typically don't include overnight breaks. As a result, elapsed time is somewhat higher than that of over-the-road drivers, with an average speed of 34.9 mph and a median of 36.1 mph.

The Effect of Satellite Systems on Miles, Earnings, Safety, and Efficiency

Satellite systems have spread rapidly throughout the freight industry: 30.7% of drivers reported having a satellite system on their truck. The previous discussion of technology indicated that truckboard communications technologies were favored by drivers because they reduce the need to stop to communicate with dispatchers. Such systems may also aid efficiency by providing information on truck locations, thereby improving dispatching. We examined these issues by comparing measures of efficiency and work life between drivers who had satellite systems and those who did not.

■ Table 28. Ratio of Miles to Reported Trip Time (mprh)

| | ALL DRIVERS | OTR | | LOCAL |
		EMPLOYEES	OWNER-OPERATORS	
Mean	52.0	54.6	51.4	40.9
Median	51.1	52.6	51.1	44.0

■ Table 29. Ratio of Miles to Elapsed Trip Time (mpeh)

| | ALL DRIVERS | OTR | | LOCAL |
		EMPLOYEES	OWNER-OPERATORS	
Mean	27.6	27.4	23.4	34.9
Median	25.1	25.3	20.8	36.1

Who Has the Systems

Although 30.7% of drivers reported having a satellite systems on their trucks, the distribution of these systems varied by type of driver. While 33.6% of over-the-road drivers reported having satellite systems, only 14.0% of local drivers had such systems. This difference may reflect both better access to phones and the use of devices such as beepers and two-way radios by local drivers. Employees were more likely to have satellite systems (32.8%) than were owner-operators (24.7%).

Relation to Mileage

Satellite systems are associated with higher mileage. Median annual 1996 mileage for drivers with satellite systems was 125,000 miles, while it was 110,000 miles for those without. The same pattern holds for the various subgroups. Median mileage of employee drivers with and without the system was also 125,000 and 110,000. Median mileage for owner-operators with systems was 121,000 miles, while those without drove 110,000. Dividing our respondents by type of work and again considering median mileage, over-the-road drivers with systems drove

120,000 miles, while those without systems drove 112,500. A like comparison cannot be made for local drivers because so few had systems. In sum, the median mileage of drivers with satellite installations was 13% greater than for those without them in 1996.

Effect on Annual Earnings

The increased mileage associated with satellite systems is not reflected in the drivers' median annual earnings. Overall, drivers with a satellite system earned only slightly more in 1996 than those without a system, $36,000 compared to $35,000. This pattern holds for employee drivers, but the gains from having a satellite system are more marked for owner-operators. Those with a system reported median annual earnings of $38,000 in 1996 compared to $32,000 for those without a system. The reverse pattern is found when the drivers are divided by their type of work, over-the-road compared to local. The earnings of over-the-road drivers are higher for those without satellite systems than for those with such systems, $40,000 compared to $38,000 for 1996.

These patterns suggest that satellite systems have little influence on annual earnings, despite the higher mileage of drivers with satellite systems. It may be that satellite-equipped trucks are most common among the larger national firms. If these firms tend to employ drivers with less experience and pay them lower rates, the mileage gain from drivers with satellites would be offset by the lower pay rates and there would be little difference in the income of those with and without the systems.

Relation of Satellite Systems to Safety

The same features that can be used to affect efficiency can also be used to improve the safety performance of drivers. Better routing and dispatching and coordination with shippers could reduce delay time and avoid unrealistic schedules. Knowledge of the location of trucks and time underway should permit firms to curb those who drive in excess of ten hours without a break.

Whatever the possibilities of the systems, they do not appear to be used to improve safety performance. The proportion of the sample who

■ Table 30. Effect of Satellite Systems on Miles, Earnings, Safety, and Efficiency

		JOB		EMPLOYMENT RELATION	
ITEM	ALL DRIVERS	OTR	LOCAL	EMPLOYEES	OWNER-OPERATORS
Have System	30.7%	33.6%	14.0%	32.8%	24.7%

Annual Miles (median)

With System	125,000	120,000	*	125,000	121,000
Without System	110,000	112,500	70,000	110,000	110,000

Median Annual Earnings (net of truck expenses for owner-operators)

With System	$36,000	$38,000	*	$36,000	$38,000
Without System	$35,000	$40,000	$35,000	$35,000	$32,000

Safety Issues

	WORKED MORE HOURS THAN LOGGED?	NUMBER OF TIMES DRIVEN MORE THAN 10 HRS. (MEAN)	NEVER DOZE WHILE DRIVING	NEVER DRIVE MORE THAN 10 HRS. DUE TO:		
				TIGHT SCHEDULES	DELAYS IN: DISPATCHING	LOADING
With System	54.2%	5.9	42.7%	66.5%	45.5%	63.9%
Without System	56.5%	6.7	40.9%	68.9%	40.8%	65.1%

Loading of Truck, Deadhead Miles, and Waiting Time

		LIMITED BY				TIME ON TRIP (MEDIAN:*MEAN*)	
ITEM	DEADHEAD MILES	WEIGHT & VOLUME	WEIGHT ONLY	VOLUME ONLY	NOT LIMITED	ON-DUTY, NOT DRIVING	WAITING
All Trucks	68.9	33.0%	10.2%	18.4%	38.4%	1.5:*4.6hrs*	1.3:*2.3hrs*
With System	61.4	31.2%	5.8%	19.3%	43.7%	1.8:*4.6hrs*	1.0:*1.9hrs*
Without System	75.4	34.0%	12.1%	17.9%	36.0%	1.5:*4.7hrs*	1.5:*2.5hrs*

*Sample is too small to be reliable.

■ Figure 33. Satellite Usage and Mileage

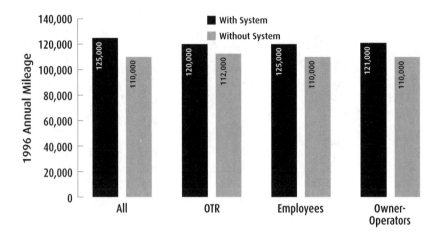

report working more hours than they logged is not substantially lower for those with systems than those without. Similarly, there is no meaningful difference in the proportion reporting they never drive more than ten hours because of tight schedules, dispatching delays, or delays in loading for those with systems and those without. The proportion who report *never* dozing while driving is likewise very similar for our two groups, 63.9% of those with systems and 65.1% of those without systems. The only substantial difference is in the number of times driving over ten hours without a break in the last thirty days. The mean value for those with systems was 5.9 times, while for those without systems it was 6.7 times.

Relation of Satellite Systems to Loading, Deadhead Miles, and Waiting Time

The closer monitoring and better communications permitted by satellite systems should allow firms to utilize their trucks more effectively. We would then expect that satellite-equipped trucks should have fewer deadhead miles, should be limited by weight or volume more often, and should have fewer unproductive hours (waiting time and on-duty non-driving time).

■ Figure 34. Satellite Usage and Annual Income

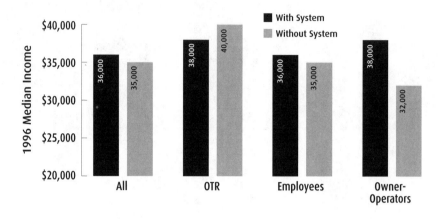

The results are mixed. Drivers with satellite systems reported fewer empty miles on their last trip: 61.4 for those with satellite systems compared to 75.4 for those without systems. Loading cuts the other way, however: trucks with satellite systems are *less* likely to be limited by weight or volume than are those without such systems: 43.7% compared to 36.0%. This difference may reflect the use of satellite systems to provide expedited or specialized services. Nondriving work time on the last trip was not greatly affected by satellite systems. Drivers with a system averaged 1.8 hours of nondriving work time on the prior trip, while those without a system averaged 1.5 hours. Median hours differed even less, by only six minutes. Differences in waiting time were more substantial and favored those with satellites. Those with systems averaged one hour of waiting time on the last trip, while those without averaged 1.5 hours of waiting time. Median hours followed a similar pattern: those with a system reported 1.9 hours, while those without reported 2.5 hours.

Conclusion

Satellite systems appear to be associated with improved efficiency, but they have little influence on drivers' work lives. There is evidence that satellites are associated with increased mileage, fewer deadhead miles and reduced waiting time. With the exception of owner-operators, however, there is little evidence that drivers with satellite systems have higher incomes or a better work life.

All of these conclusions are tentative. There may be other factors, such as firm size, influencing the outcomes. As in the discussion of driver income, firm size may be correlated with implementation of satellite systems and with efficiency of operations. Distinguishing such factors requires a more comprehensive analysis.

CHAPTER 7

Regulation and Pressures on the Job

Logbooks and Scheduling Pressures

The Hours of Service Regulations were enacted as part of the Motor Carrier Act of 1935 in response to public concerns about the overwork of drivers and the consequent hazard to both the public and the drivers. Modeled on similar regulations of railroads, these rules remained substantially unchanged until January 2004. Hours of Service Regulations are currently enforced by the Office of Motor Carriers of the U.S. Department of Transportation.

The substantive requirements of the Hours of Service Regulations have been discussed in the chapter on working hours. Most drivers are required to keep a log of their driving time, on-duty nondriving time, and rest breaks. This log, typically a paper record, must be kept up to date. It is available to law enforcement officers and state and federal transportation inspectors. Drivers are responsible for obeying the Hours of Service Regulations, and they, rather than freight firms or shippers, are liable for violations.[1] Although enforcement varies by state, Hours of Service Regulations are generally held to be weakly enforced. The continued use of self-recorded paper logs stands in contrast to the technological advances that have occurred elsewhere in the industry.

The driver survey asked a series of questions about the drivers' use and the accuracy of their logbooks. These questions included whether the drivers used a logbook, whether their logbooks were accurate, whether they had worked more hours than they had recorded in the last thirty days, if they had driven more than ten hours without an eight-hour break, why they had done so and the typical reasons drivers exceeded the ten-hour rule, and whether they had dozed while driving in the last thirty days. As some of these questions involved admission of violations of the Hours of Service Regulations, some underreporting is to be expected.

Use and Accuracy of Logbooks

Ninety-four percent (94%) of respondents used logbooks. This included 99% of over-the-road drivers but only 67% of local drivers. Most of those not using logs worked in positions, such as construction truck driver, that did not involve freight hauling.

Drivers were asked whether they thought that logbooks accurately reflected hours of work for most drivers, and whether they had worked more hours than recorded in their log in the last thirty days. Only 16.1% of the sample responded that they believe that logbooks reflect actual hours of work. Owner-operators were least likely to believe logs were accurate (11.4%), and local drivers were most likely to believe that logs were accurate (23.1%), but these differences are overshadowed by over-all agreement that logs are not accurate.

A majority of drivers, 55.8%, indicated that they had worked more hours than they had recorded in their logbooks in the last thirty days. Local drivers were least likely to report under-recording hours. Only 30.5% indicated that they had done so. In contrast, almost 60% of over-the-road employees and owner-operators reported working more than they had recorded at least once in the last thirty days.

Violations of Hours of Service Regulations

How often do drivers drive more than ten hours without an eight-hour break? Nearly forty-five percent (44.8%) of respondents reported that they had not driven more than ten hours without a break in the last thirty days. Those driving excessive hours one to five times in the past thirty days were 23.4% of the sample, those driving more than ten hours six to ten times during this period were 11.2% of the sample, eleven to fifteen

■ Figure 35. Accuracy of Logbooks

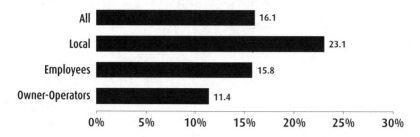

■ Figure 36. Worked More Hours than Logged in the Past Thirty Days

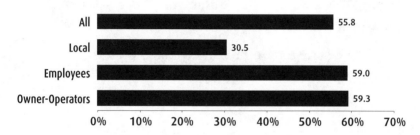

times were 4.5% of the sample, while those exceeding the limits of sixteen or more times in the last thirty days were 16.2% of the sample.

Two questions were asked about why drivers violated Hours of Service Regulations. First, why the respondent drove more than ten hours, and second, the most common reasons why drivers violated the Hours of Service Regulations. Respondents reported that when *they* drove more than ten hours, it was often because of a tight schedule (23.1%), traffic delays (21%), delays in loading or unloading (19%), or a desire to make more money (16.7%) (table 31, figure 39). Fewer drivers reported dispatch delays (6.7%) or weather (7.7%) as a frequent cause of their driving more than ten hours. The Hours of Service Regulations provide exceptions to the ten-hour rule when drivers are near their destination and have been delayed by traffic or weather (if the delay is unexpected).

A similar pattern is apparent when respondents are asked to list the most common reasons why drivers violate the Hours of Service

■ **Table 31. Number of Times in Last Thirty Days Drove more than Ten Hours without an Eight-Hour Break**

TIMES	ALL	LOCAL	EMPLOYEES	OWNER-OPERATORS
0	44.8%	72.3%	41.8%	39.0%
1–5	23.4%	10.8%	23.2%	29.8%
6–10	11.2%	4.6%	13.2%	9.2%
11–15	4.5%	3.1%	4.9%	4.3%
16+	16.2%	9.2%	16.9%	17.7%

■ **Figure 37. Reasons Cited as "Often" the Cause for Driving more than Ten Hours by Type of Driver**

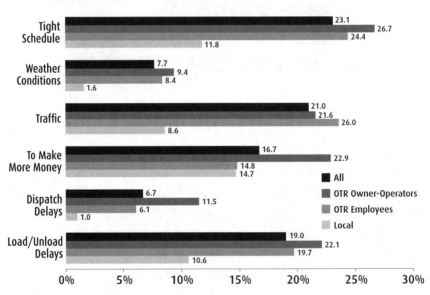

Regulations. The most frequently cited reasons are to make more money (25.3%), because shippers set unrealistic requirements on deliveries (20.6%), to complete a job (9.6%), due to dispatcher pressure (8.3%), because of delays in loading and unloading (6.6%), and because driving hours are not long enough (5.4%).

■ Table 32. Reasons for Driving more than Ten Hours

	ALL	LOCAL	EMPLOYEES	OWNER-OPERATORS
Tight Schedule				
Often	23.1%	11.8%	24.4%	26.7%
Sometimes	35.6%	24.1%	38.5%	35.2%
Never	41.3%	64.2%	37.2%	38.1%
Weather Conditions				
Often	7.7%	1.6%	8.4%	9.4%
Sometimes	46.3%	43.0%	49.6%	41.3%
Never	45.8%	55.4%	42.1%	49.3%
Traffic				
Often	21.0%	8.6%	23.6%	21.6%
Sometimes	44.8%	42.5%	46.9%	41.5%
Never	34.2%	49.0%	29.5%	36.9%
To Make More Money				
Often	16.7%	14.7%	14.8%	22.9%
Sometimes	15.8%	18.7%	15.5%	15.2%
Never	67.6%	66.7%	69.8%	61.9%
Dispatch Delays				
Often	6.7%	1.0%	6.1%	11.5%
Sometimes	25.8%	22.0%	28.5%	20.4%
Never	67.7%	77.0%	65.4%	68.1%
Load/Unload Delays				
Often	19.0%	10.6%	19.7%	22.1%
Sometimes	39.0%	36.7%	40.6%	36.8%
Never	42.0%	52.7%	39.7%	41.2%

Response to Unrealistic Schedules and Penalties for Arriving Late

Drivers indicate that unrealistic schedules set by freight firms and shippers are an important cause of violations of the ten-hour rule. The majority of drivers (57.5%) reported that they respond to such requests by renegotiating the time, 33.5% reported that they take the load but do

■ Table 33. Response to Unrealistic Schedule and Penalties for Arriving Late

	ALL	LOCAL	EMPLOYEES		OWNER-OPERATORS
			UNION	NONUNION	(NONUNION)
Response to Unrealistic Schedule					
Renegotiate Time	57.5%	51.3%	44.0%	59.1%	57.8%
Don't Change Time/Speed	33.5%	31.5%	32.0%	36.5%	32.4%
Refuse Load	14.3%	11.2%	14.3%	12.6%	19.7%
Drive Faster/More Hours	15.5%	11.2%	8.0%	15.5%	17.4%
Penalties for Arriving Late					
Disciplined	36.4%	28.0%	36.7%	39.6%	31.8%
Lose Work	30.6%	17.5%	22.0%	27.3%	39.0%
Pay Reduced	7.6%	4.7%	2.0%	5.5%	15.3%

not change their speed or time for the trip, 14.3% reported that they refuse the load, and 15.5% reported that they drive faster or for more hours.

The pattern of response varies by type of driver. Owner-operators are the most likely to refuse a load (19.7%) but also somewhat more likely to driver faster or for more hours (17.4%).[2] Nonunion employees are slightly more likely than owner-operators to renegotiate the time (59.1%), least likely to refuse a load (12.6%), and most likely to not change their speed or time (15.5%). The pattern of response is different for union employees. They are the least likely to driver faster (8.0%) but are also the least likely to renegotiate the time (44.0%) and are about as likely to refuse a load (14.3%) or drive without changing speed or time (32.0%) as other types of drivers. This pattern of response may reflect both a lower probability of being given an unrealistic schedule in the union sector of the industry and a greater ability to resist unrealistic schedules. Local drivers' responses to the questions on unrealistic schedules fall below those of the full sample, suggesting that they are faced with such scheduling less frequently than over-the-road drivers. As in other cases, this likely reflects differences in the work of local and over-the-road drivers.

An important element in driver response to scheduling is how they are penalized when they do not meet their schedule. More than one-third of the respondents (36.4%) reported that they would receive a disciplinary warning or suspension if they arrived late for a pickup or drop. Somewhat more than thirty percent (30.6%) reported that they would lose work by missing a dispatch or getting a bad dispatch, and a small number (7.6% of the sample) reported that they would have their pay reduced.

The pattern of penalties varies by type of employee. Nonunion employees were the most likely to be disciplined (39.6%). Nonunion owner-operators were the most likely to lose work (39.0%) and to have their pay reduced (15.3%) but less likely to be disciplined (31.8%). Union employees ran a slightly lower risk (36.7%) of discipline than nonunion employees, and were less likely to lose work (22.0%) or have their pay reduced (2.0%).

Pressures on Drivers

The responses to the questions on why drivers violate the ten-hour rule indicate that they are both pushed and pulled toward such behavior. First, employers and shippers push drivers to drive in excess of ten hours by setting schedules that require excessive hours or speed. Although drivers report renegotiating such schedules or ignoring unrealistic schedules, they are subject to discipline when they do not meet their schedules. It also seems doubtful that a freight firm would retain a driver who regularly renegotiated his or her schedule or ignored assigned schedules. On the pull side, drivers' pay rates are low and, as this report shows, they have to work 150% of the normal full-time year to earn a middle-class income. One means of improving their earnings is to drive extended days to "make more money." This is further encouraged by firms that penalize late drivers by delaying dispatches or assigning bad dispatches. Placing sole liability for violations of limits on driving time on drivers, rather than also allocating it to firms and shippers, also encourages the latter to largely ignore the consequences of their demands.

Drowsiness While Driving

One regular topic of conversation among interviewers was how tired many of the respondents appeared to be during the interview. More than a few became visibly sleepy or dozed during interviews, even after drinking a cup of coffee. Dozing during an interview is not a problem, but dozing while driving a truck can be. Drivers were asked how many times they had dozed or fallen asleep while driving a truck in the last thirty days. The majority of drivers, 64.3%, reported that they had not dozed during that period. Of the remaining 35.7%, 7.3% reported dozing once, 13% reported dozing twice, 8.1% reported dozing three to four times, and 7.3% reported dozing more than four times in the last thirty days. These results suggest that the image of large numbers of drivers dozing while driving down highways, made popular in some television reports, is overstated. Most drivers do not doze while driving, and those who have dozed do not do so often. Nevertheless, dozing while driving is not uncommon among drivers and represents a significant hazard to the driver as well as to others. Finding ways of lessening delivery pressures and providing additional rest areas might do much to reduce the frequency of dozing while driving.

Changes to Hours of Service Regulations

Drivers were asked about the changes they would like made to the Hours of Service Regulations. The most frequent proposal was to have on-duty non-driving time counted differently. Recall that often when drivers are waiting to have their trailer loaded or unloaded or to get into a dock they are resting or completing paperwork. Thus, they feel they should be "off the clock" for this time. Many drivers stated that they could not keep logbooks honest and also complete dispatches if they accurately counted all their on-duty nondriving time.

Approximately 18% of drivers stated that they should be allowed to drive more than ten hours before having to take a break. A number

■ Figure 38. Times Dozed while Driving in Past Thirty Days

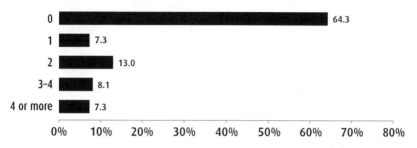

■ Table 34. Top Five Proposed Hours of Service Regulation Changes

Count on-duty hours differently than driving hours	28.3%
Able to drive more than ten hours at a time	17.6%
Return to seventy hours of driving time after a twenty-four-hour break	8.0%
Change logbook	7.3%
Higher pay/get paid differently	5.7%

wanted to be allowed to drive twelve hours, arguing that this would allow them to take advantage of daylight driving hours and that they could then take their break at night.

Eight percent cited the need to re-evaluate the seventy-hour rule. Under this rule, drivers are limited to seventy hours of work in an eight-day period. The eight-day period is not a fixed period but covers the current day and the seven previous days. Thus, the seventy-hour/eight-day constraint is constantly measured and involves, from the point of view of many drivers, fairly complex record keeping and calculations. Many drivers proposed that they start with a fresh seventy hours after a twenty-four-hour break from work.

Some Suggestions about the Hours of Service Regulations

On January 4, 2004, the U.S. Department of Transportation implemented revised Hours of Service Regulations. These new regulations, which were subject to extensive review by the industry and by drivers, have incorporated some of the driver suggests found in the driver survey. Drivers are now allowed eleven hours of driving or fourteen hours of total work time before a ten-hour break. There is also a restart provision which allows drivers to begin new sixty and seventy hour cycles after thirty-four continuous hours off duty. The new regulations are more restrictive in that drivers are required to take their ten-hour break fourteen hours after beginning work even if they have spent some of those hours off duty. This contrasts with the previous regulations that allowed drivers to use off duty time to extend the length of their work day. Taken together, these revisions represent a step toward limiting drivers' hours of work while increasing their ability to make a living from their work. It also moves drivers closer to working on a twenty-four hour cycle that better fits the rhythms of the human body. There are still problems inherent in the revised regulations.

Drivers are not aided economically by a revision that increases total hours of driving time. Truck drivers work 150% of the typical full-time work year, based upon a forty-hour criterion, working far in excess of what we, as a nation, hold to be a reasonable work week. Low earnings and long hours have created a dynamic in which drivers work additional hours to raise their earnings. Yet the extra supply of labor created by long hours holds rates down and encourages drivers to work even more hours. Extending driving hours may make the driver's condition worse by reinforcing both the increase in hours and the decline in effective mileage rates.

The new regulations continue to hold drivers liable for violations of Hours of Service, which does not deter shippers and freight firms from setting unrealistic delivery schedules. An important reform would be the allocation of liability for violations of the Hours of Service Regulations among all of those responsible for the trip schedule. This would provide incentives for shippers and carriers to develop more realistic schedules and insist that their drivers adhere to the regulations.

Finally, the new regulations do little to improve enforcement of the Hours of Service Regulations. It is well known to the important players in the industry, the shippers, carriers, and regulators, that drivers regularly violate the regulations. The system of paper logs permits use of multiple logs to conceal these violations. Many drivers told interviewers that they carried multiple logs, and a few showed the interviewers the logs they were currently running. More than one driver expressed the view that the lack of any effort, such as putting serial numbers on logbooks to prevent the use of multiple logs, indicates that neither the carriers nor the regulators are really concerned about drivers' hours of work. Given the advent of sophisticated technologies capable of onboard and remote monitoring, it is possible to develop a system that could be less subject to misreporting. Such technologies are available and required in other countries. It should certainly be possible to implement some system that assures accurate reporting of hours in the United States.

Stricter enforcement of the Hours of Service Regulations would help drivers by reducing the effective labor supply, thereby raising mileage rates. Drivers would be able to work fewer hours to achieve reasonable earnings. This would also protect their health and the safety of the public. Requiring hourly pay for on-duty nondriving time would also help drivers, as it would provide pay for currently uncompensated work time. Firms and shippers would be encouraged to use drivers' time efficiently. This would also decrease the incentive to conceal on-duty nondriving time.

CHAPTER 8

How the Driver Views His Job

Views of the Job

In addition to asking questions that measure outcomes such as rates of pay, mileage, hours, and gender, drivers were asked more "subjective" questions about how they felt about their occupation, about their firms, and about labor unions. These questions allowed drivers to express their opinions about their jobs. Some of these questions presented drivers with a specific issue and asked for a graded response, while others were open ended, permitting the drivers to discuss the issue. These less structured questions allowed drivers to determine what was important, from their point of view.

Driving as a Career Job

Although some drivers remain in their occupation for many years, this does not necessarily mean that they are satisfied with the nature of their work. The high turnover and quit rates give evidence that drivers are not satisfied with their jobs. One measure of job satisfaction is whether an individual would *want* to continue his or her current work. Drivers were first asked whether they would *like* to be working as a driver in five years. Nearly sixty-six percent (66.2%) of drivers answered affirmatively to this question. Owner-operators were most likely to want to continue (71.0%), followed closely by union employees (69.8%) and then by nonunion employees (63.4%). Those who responded positively where

■ Figure 39. Career Commitment by Type of Employment

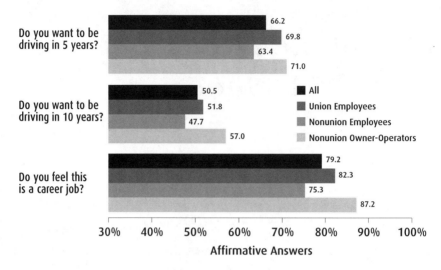

then asked whether they would *like* to be working as a driver in ten years. Half (50.5%) answered affirmatively, with 57% of owner-operators, 51.8% of union employees, and 47.7% of nonunion employees answering yes. Overall, two-thirds of the sample would like to still be driving in five years, one-half of these would like to still be driving in ten years. The lower response to the ten-year question reflects, in part, that some drivers planned to retire within ten years. Nevertheless, it was substantially lower than the five-year response.

Another question that addressed the drivers' view of the job was whether the respondent felt that driving was a career job, "one you could do until you retire." This is a somewhat different approach, as it is not asking if the drivers would *like* to be driving until they retire, but rather whether they believed they *could* drive until they retired. Most drivers view driving as a job they can continue. Nearly eighty percent (79.2%) of the entire sample, 82.3% of union employees, 75.3% of nonunion employees, and 87.2% of owner-operators responded in the affirmative. This suggests that drivers do not believe that the physical demands of the job will prevent them from continuing to work as drivers until they leave the labor force.

Likes and Dislikes

At the end of the interview, a series of open-ended questions asked drivers what they enjoyed most about their job, what they disliked most, and what they found most challenging. Much in keeping with the image of drivers, 35.5% of drivers reported that they liked the independence and freedom that driving afforded them. Nearly thirty-one percent (31.1%) reported that they liked seeing the country and different sights. The third-most-common response (12.9%) was that they enjoyed driving.

Turning to what drivers liked least about their work, 27.7% responded that being away from home and family was the worst thing. Nearly eighteen percent (18.2%) of all drivers reported that they least enjoyed things such as night driving, driving on rough roads, and bad drivers. This was followed by time spent waiting (for loads, dispatches, etc.), with 7.8% of drivers citing this as a dislike.

Table 35. Job Satisfaction

What do you enjoy most about your work?

Independence; freedom; "being my own boss"	35.5%
Seeing the country; seeing different sights	31.1%
Driving; "it's fun"	12.9%

What do you enjoy least about your work?

Being away from home and family; hours spent alone	27.7%
Driving conditions; bad drivers; rough roads; night driving	18.2%
Waiting for loads; down time; waiting for work	7.8%

What is most challenging about your work?

Time schedules; dealing with shippers and receivers; keeping customer happy	19.7%
Driving in major cities; holiday traffic	16.3%
Putting up with other drivers; "four-wheelers are dangerous"	13.1%

Note: The percentages are given for the top three responses as a percentage of those who responded. All statistics are calculated with weights proportional to probability of appearing in sample.

Nearly twenty percent (19.7%) of drivers reported that the time schedules and keeping shippers and receivers happy were the most challenging parts of their work. This was followed closely by the demands of driving in big cities and dealing with holiday traffic (16.3%). Finally, 13.1% of drivers reported that dealing with other drivers, specifically automobile drivers, was the most challenging part of their work.

View of Employers

What do drivers think about their employers? The survey presented drivers with a series of questions regarding their company's concern about nine aspects of their work life. For owner-operators these questions would concern the firms to which they were permanently leased. These questions were adapted from a larger battery of questions asked of over-the-road drivers in a survey by the Upper Great Plains Transportation Research Center.

Table 36. Views of Employers

| | ALL DRIVERS | EMPLOYEES | | OWNER-OPERATORS |
		UNION	NONUNION	(NONUNION)
Your company is very concerned about your need for:				
Improving your income	27.9%	18.1%	28.8%	30.0%
Fringe benefits	20.6%	21.3%	23.8%	12.6%
Time at home; well-being of family	46.9%	44.3%	51.0%	36.6%
Safety, quality, and maintenance of equipment	79.1%	68.0%	80.6%	79.7%
Not wasting your time	39.8%	37.0%	45.3%	26.0%
An accurate paycheck	68.2%	65.8%	69.7%	64.9%
Safe working conditions	59.5%	54.9%	60.4%	58.4%
Protecting your health	53.3%	52.0%	55.0%	48.9%
Having a secure and stable job	57.3%	52.8%	59.9%	52.0%

Note: The percentages are for the respondents who reported that their company was very concerned about that particular issue.

These questions were scaled from very concerned, to somewhat concerned, to not concerned at all. Most drivers reported that their firms were very concerned about the safety, quality, and maintenance of equipment: 79.1% of all drivers, 68% of union employees, 80.6% of nonunion employees, and 79.7% of owner-operators. Companies also earned high marks on accurate paychecks, with 68.2% of all drivers reporting that their companies were very concerned about this issue.

In contrast, drivers were not positive about their companies' concerns with pay or benefits. Only 27.9% of all drivers stated that their companies were very concerned about improving their income, and only 20.6% reported that their companies were very concerned about fringe benefits. Union drivers believed their companies were less concerned with improving their income than did nonunion employees (18.1% versus 28.8%). This may reflect union members' perception that the union wins benefits from firms.

Drivers' views of their firms with regard to family matters fell between the prior results. Nearly forty-seven percent (46.9%) of all drivers said their companies were concerned about their time at home. This figure was lowest for owner-operators, with only 36.6% reporting their companies were very concerned. Fewer than forty percent (39.8%) of employees reported that their companies were very concerned about not wasting their time. Again, this figure was lowest for owner-operators (26.0%), the group least likely to be paid for nondriving time or time waiting for dispatches on the road.

View of Unions

The International Brotherhood of Teamsters (IBT) played a central role in the over-the-road freight industry from the mid-1930s until the 1980s. The organization of over-the-road drivers and consolidation of labor agreements into the National Master Freight Agreement in the 1960s gave the union, and its members, considerable control over the terms and conditions of work. Drivers achieved their highest rate of pay, both in real dollars and relative to other employees, in the 1960s and 1970s, the era when the Teamsters were at the height of their bargaining power. Deregulation and deunionization, among other factors, have greatly decreased the role of unions in the motor freight industry in recent years.

Drivers were asked two types of questions about unions. First, they were presented a series of statements about how a driver's work would be affected if the union played a larger role in the industry. Drivers were asked to respond to the statements using a four-point Likert scale that ran from strongly agree to strongly disagree. The questions covered issues on which unions are generally viewed as having positive effects, and issues on which unions are typically viewed negatively. The second question asked whether the driver would shift to an organized firm if offered the opportunity.

What do respondents believe would happen if more drivers became union members and the union played a larger role in the industry? Most drivers' views of unions are positive. More than two-thirds of the respondents agreed or strongly agreed that driver's earnings would increase (72.4%) and more drivers would have good health insurance and pensions (79.7%). Somewhat over half believed that drivers would work fewer hours (53.4%), and somewhat under half agreed the job would be safer (44.2%). On the negative side, drivers also believed that conflict between employees and employers would increase (76.3%) and that there would be strikes (86.5%). A substantial proportion, almost sixty percent (57.3%) agreed that nothing would change but union officials would get rich. Despite such negatives, a majority of respondents, 59.9%, agreed that drivers would be better off if the union were stronger.

The pattern of responses differed by the type of employment relationship. Union employees' views of unions were more positive than those of nonmembers. Almost all union employees agreed that a more powerful union would improve earnings and benefits and that drivers would be better off. Three-quarters (76.5%) of union members agreed that a more powerful union would mean that the job would be safer, and two-thirds agreed that it would mean that drivers would work fewer hours (67.4%). Although union members agreed that there would be

■ Figure 40. What Drivers Predict If the Union Played a Larger Role by Type of Employment

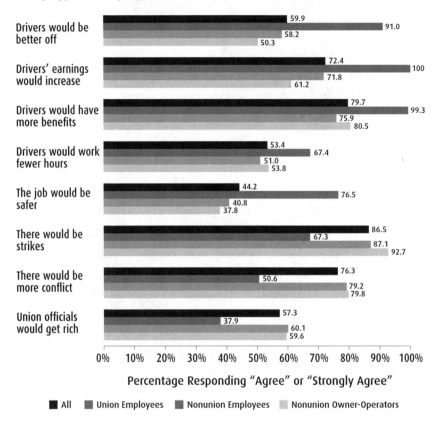

Percentage Responding "Agree" or "Strongly Agree"

■ All ■ Union Employees ■ Nonunion Employees ■ Nonunion Owner-Operators

more conflict (50.6%) and strikes (67.3%), only slightly over one-third (37.9%) agreed that little would change but union officials would get rich. Given the perception of corruption in the IBT, the favorable attitude of union respondents toward their union reflects some success in the reform efforts of the last decade.

The views of nonmembers, both employees and owner-operators, are less favorable. Sixty percent or more of nonunion employees and owner-operators agreed that a stronger union would improve driver earnings (71.8% for employees, 61.2% for owner-operators) and benefits (75.9% and 80.5%, respectively, for employees and owner-operators). About half

■ **Figure 41. Whether Drivers Would Work for a Union Firm**

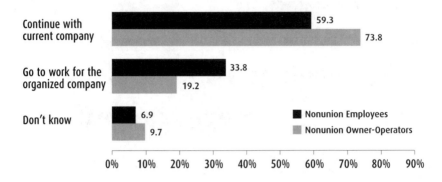

agreed that employees would work fewer hours per week (51.0% and 53.8%, respectively), and about 40% agreed that the job would be safer (40.8% for employees, 37.8% for owner-operators). Nonmembers were more likely to agree with the negative statements about unions. Almost 80% of each group agreed there would be more conflict, and about 90% agreed that there would be more strikes. Sixty percent of the nonmember respondents agreed that nothing would change but union officials would become rich. Despite the strength of the negative response, nonmember drivers generally agreed that drivers would be better off if the union were stronger (58.2% for nonunion employees and 50.3% for nonunion owner-operators).

Would nonunion drivers shift to an organized company if they were offered the opportunity? Variants on this question have been asked in most surveys on unionization, but often implicitly have involved assessments of whether the respondent would participate in an attempt to organize his or her firm. We asked drivers to assume that conditions were similar between their current job and a unionized position and then reflect on whether they would shift jobs. Most nonunion employees (59.3%) and owner-operators (73.8%) responded they would continue with their current firm. A substantial proportion, 33.8% of employees and 19.2% of owner-operators, stated that they would shift over. The numbers for employees are similar to those for the national labor force, where about one-third of nonmembers express a desire to work for a unionized employer.

The results from the two sets of questions on unions indicate that, although many nonmembers have reservations about unions, half or more have a positive view of what unions can do for drivers and a quarter to a third would prefer to work for an organized firm even if the terms and conditions of work were similar to those at their current position.

Musical Preferences of Drivers

Finally, truck drivers have long had a reputation of strongly preferring country western music, perhaps reflecting an identification with cowboys and western imagery. At the end of the interview we asked drivers

■ Figure 42. Musical Preferences of OTR Drivers

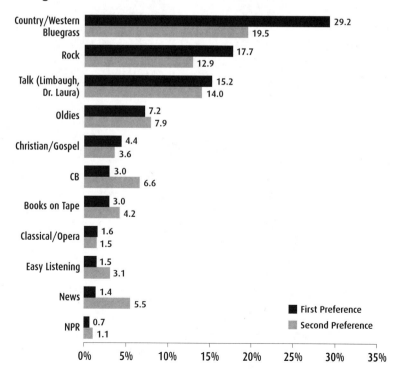

their preferences in radio programming. The interviewers reported that the drivers enjoyed discussing the topic and that many reported broad programming interests. Nevertheless, the drivers' core preferences stood out clearly: they do enjoy country western more than other programming. This is, to the knowledge of all with whom we have discussed the issue, the "scientific" study of this topic. We are pleased that even if this study has eroded some of the misconceptions about truck drivers, we have established a factual basis for this long-standing belief.

Sample Design for a Study of U.S. Truck Drivers

Judith H. Connor and Steven G. Heeringa

Introduction

The Sloan Foundation Trucking Industry Project (TIP) is an inter-university research project that studies issues relating to the trucking industry in the United States. Researchers on this project are from the University of Michigan, the University of Wisconsin in Milwaukee, and the University of Massachusetts.

In order to better understand trucking jobs and trucking companies, TIP conducted a survey of truck drivers in five Midwestern states: Illinois, Indiana, Michigan, Ohio, and Wisconsin. The study, which is funded by the Sloan Foundation, asked about details of trucking jobs and the lifestyle of truck drivers. This information will help government and other researchers understand what life on the road is like. Although the study is initially limited to the five Midwestern states, it is hoped that this study will serve as a pilot for a larger national survey of truck drivers.

The TIP staff asked the University of Michigan's Survey Research Center (SRC) for help in planning the survey and designing and selecting the sample of truck drivers. Survey specialists from the SRC Division of Surveys and Technologies (DST) consulted on the questionnaire design and conducted interviewer training. DST programmers set up the sample management systems that were used in monitoring the progress of the study. Steven Heeringa, a sampling statistician and Director of DST, designed a probability sampling methodology that enabled the researchers to collect data in a cost-efficient way from a representative sample of truck drivers. Because a probability sampling design was used, the results of this pilot study are projectable to the survey population—truck drivers in the states of Illinois, Indiana, Michigan, Ohio, and Wisconsin.

The following sections describe the sample design for the TIP study. They offer an overview of the multi-stage sample design, a description of the selection of the first stage sampling units (the twenty truck stops); the selection of the days of the week and times of the day to be sampled at each truck stop; the third stage selection of individual truck drivers; and the construction of sampling weights.

Overview of Multi-Stage Sample Design

The TIP researchers wanted to interview approximately 650 truck drivers. Because the truckers' work schedules keep them on the road for days at a time, telephone interviews or face-to-face interviews at their homes were considered impractical. Methods for sampling the drivers through trucking organizations, places of employment, weigh stations, or truck stops were considered. Among the factors considered were the availability of a sampling frame or list (or the feasibility of constructing one); the coverage (proportion of truck drivers included) of the sampling frame; the availability of a measure of size (MOS) indicating the relative number of truck drivers associated with each element in the proposed sampling frame; and the practicality of sampling truck drivers and conducting interviews at each sampled location. It was decided that for ease of administration and cost efficiency, the face-to-face interviews should be clustered by location and time of day. Taking all of these factors into consideration, truck stops were chosen as the first-stage units of selection.

A multi-stage sample design is used in this project. The overall sample design consisted of a first-stage selection of truck stops, a second-stage selection of days of the week and times of the day to administer the survey at each truck stop, and a third-stage selection of individual truck drivers. At each stage of selection, the probability of selection was known and a method was in place for ensuring the randomness of the sample selection process. A similar methodology was developed by Steven Heeringa and used by SRC to draw a sample of University of Michigan Library users.

Factors that influenced the decision about the number of truck stops to select included the level of staffing available, the length of the field period, and the balance between cost and sampling error considerations. While it is less costly to staff a smaller number of first-stage sampling units (truck stops), if the number of first-stage units is too small, the level of sampling error for estimates is unacceptably high. A sample of twenty truck stops was found to have satisfactory cost and error properties. To reach the desired sample size of 650 respondents, 32–33 interviews were planned per truck stop.

There were two teams of interviewers working at two truck stops on any given day. The teams consisted of one SRC interviewer and five TIP interviewers. One team was based in Ann Arbor and one was based in Wisconsin. The production interviewing period was from late July through the middle of September 1997. Sample design assumptions called for twenty-five regular (about forty-five minute) interviews per truck stop, resulting in five hundred full-length interviews. While most of these interviews were collected at truck stops, truckers had the option to schedule a telephone interview at a time that would be convenient. In addition, short-form interviews were offered to drivers who were selected for but refused the regular interview. The short, five-minute interviews were designed to collect demographic and other critical information to aid in nonresponse adjustments. It was expected that there would be 150–200 short interviews (8–10 short interviews per truck stop) from drivers who refused the regular interview. The mix of the interviews could be from 450 long/200 short to 500 long/150 short for a total of 650 truck stop interviews.

There was also a second sample of truck drivers selected at the fuel line. The purpose of this sample was to interview drivers who only stop for fuel but do not enter the truck stop. The drivers who stop only for fuel may have different characteristics, issues, and concerns from those who enter the truck stop to rest or have a meal. Including interviews from both groups was expected to give more complete coverage of the truck driver population. There were to be twenty-five short fuel line interviews per truck stop for a total of five-hundred fuel-line interviews. These five-minute interviews would be conducted during the first hour of a shift and would involve only one interviewer, who would be responsible for both sampling and interviewing. Overall, a total of 1,150 interviews were desired—650 from the truck stops and 500 from the fuel lines.

First Stage: Selection of Truck Stops

A total of twenty truck stops were selected with probability proportional to size (PPS) from the *ValuList* national data base of truck stops compiled from the 1997 edition of *The Trucker's Friend: The National Truck Stop Directory*. The machine readable version of the directory, TRUXTOPS.DBF, has listings for 5,204 U.S. truck stops and includes 88 data elements for each truck stop listing. Data elements available include the name, address, fuel brand, telephone number, credit cards accepted, and information about the facilities and services. One of the available data fields, the number of overnight truck parking spaces, was suitable to use for a measure of size (MOS) because it is available for almost all of the truck stops and it provides some indication of the relative number of truck drivers who visit each truck stop.

The sampling frame of truck stops was limited to truck stops in Illinois, Indiana, Michigan, Ohio, and Wisconsin that had at least one overnight truck parking space. The truck stops differ greatly by size— ranging from sites with fewer than ten spaces to sites with more than two hundred overnight parking spaces. In order to ensure that the distribution of parking spaces in the sample of twenty truck stops matched the bivariate distribution of spaces by state and size category in the population, a controlled selection technique was used to select the truck stops. Controlled selection is a probability sampling technique that incorporates distributional controls on sample elements beyond those which are built in to the sample design explicitly through stratification.

The truck stops were grouped into six size categories according to the number of overnight truck parking spaces: 1–9, 10–24, 25–49, 50–99, 100–199, and 200+. Table 1 shows the distribution by size category and state. Each cell of the table has three lines. The first line shows the proportion of truck stops which fall into the size category by state cell; the second line shows the expected number of selections from the cell which would occur in a sample of 20 truck stops; and the third line shows the number of truck stops actually selected from the cell. For example, in the cell for truck stops with 100–199 parking spaces in the State of Illinois, the first line shows that the proportion of truck stops in the five-state area that fall into this cell is 0.0718, and in a sample of 20 truck stops, 0.0718 × 20 or 1.436 truck stops are expected to be selected. This means that there should be either 1 or 2 truck stops selected. The controlled selection algorithm enforces this constraint. The third line shows that two truck stops were actually selected from this cell.

The controlled selection program generated a set thirty patterns of possible numbers of selections of truck stops by cell—each of which satisfied the constraints of the two-way table. Each pattern has an associated probability or measure of size (MOS) related to the combined probabilities of the cell selections. The sum of the probabilities of all the possible patterns is 1.0. One pattern was selected with probability proportional to the size (PPS). Table 1 shows the distribution of truck stops by size category and state in the selected pattern (Pattern 9).

Once this distribution was determined, the number of truck stops indicated by Pattern 9 was selected with probability proportional to the number of overnight truck parking spaces (PPS) from the set of all truck stops in each state by size class cell. This procedure resulted in a first-stage sample of twenty truck stops.

Second Stage: Selection of Days of Week and Times of Day

In order to have the most complete coverage of the truck driver population, it was important to conduct interviewing all seven days of the

■ Table 1. Allocation of Sample Using Controlled Selection

STATE	NUMBER OF PARKING SPACES FOR TRUCKS (MOS)						
	1–9	10–24	25–49	50–99	100–199	200+	TOTAL
IL	0.0018	0.0074	0.0116	0.0407	0.0718	0.0682	0.2016
	0.034	0.148	0.232	0.814	1.436	1.364	4.028
	0	0	0	1	2	1	4
IN	0.0015	0.0110	0.0212	0.0652	0.1010	0.0586	0.2585
	0.030	0.220	0.424	1.304	2.020	1.172	5.170
	0	1	0	1	2	1	5
MI	0.0020	0.0190	0.0226	0.232	0.0418	0.0342	0.1427
	0.040	0.380	0.452	0.464	0.836	0.684	2.856
	0	0	1	1	1	0	3
OH	0.0014	0.0093	0.0204	0.0561	0.0932	0.0628	0.2432
	0.028	0.186	0.408	1.122	1.864	1.256	4.864
	0	0	0	1	2	2	5
WI	0.0035	0.0133	0.0160	0.0498	0.0472	0.0243	0.1541
	0.070	0.266	0.320	0.996	0.944	0.486	3.092
	0	0	1	1	0	1	3
Total	0.0101	0.0600	0.0917	0.2349	0.3550	0.2482	1.0000
	0.202	1.200	1.836	4.700	7.100	4.962	20.000
	0	1	2	5	7	5	20

week and all times of the day when truck drivers are likely to visit the truck stops. Interviewers would work three hour shifts beginning at 5:00 A.M. This starting time was changed to 6:00 A.M. during the field period.

No interviewing was conducted during the period from 1:00 A.M. to 5:00 A.M., because that range was expected to be very unproductive due to the low volume of trucks entering the truck stops in the very early morning. At each of the twenty selected truck stops, interviews were collected on two weekdays and one weekend day.

The field period began the week of July 20th and lasted until the end of September 1997. Although the scheduling of the week assigned for interviewing at each of the truck stops was not randomized, the choice of two weekdays and one weekend day was randomly assigned to each truck stop. It was assumed that the calendar weeks were interchangeable but the volume of activity and the types of drivers could vary by day of the week. The assignment of three-hour shifts by truck stop and by day of the week was also randomly assigned. Both the days of weeks and the time of day dimensions were assigned by a systematic sampling technique in which the shifts are assigned in a systematic order beginning with a random start. Therefore all combinations of time shift by day of the week were covered and were chosen in approximately equal numbers.

Schedules of six (three per day), seven (four one day and three the second day) and eight (four per day) weekday interviewing shifts were developed for each site. The six shift schedule was ultimately chosen because the greater number of shifts were too demanding for the number of interviewers available.

Third Stage: Selection of Truck Drivers

The sample design called for approximately equal numbers of truck drivers to be interviewed at each truck stop. In order to collect a total of five hundred interviews, it was planned to take about twenty-five interviews at each truck stop.

If a measure of size (MOS) for the volume of truck drivers entering each truck stop at each time interval were known, the third stage sampling rate could be computed so that it was inversely proportional to the MOS. In this design, the MOS used to select the truck stops was the number of overnight parking spaces for trucks. This measure was expected to be correlated with the volume of truck drivers entering the truck stop.Because the MOS for the volume of truck drivers was unknown, the sampling interval was empirically determined by the number of interviews that a fixed number of interviewers working a fixed number of hours could accommodate. At busier truck stops, the third-stage sampling rate needed to be smaller; at less busy truck stops, the sampling rate was higher.

Operationally, this rate was set by the use of counting sheets. Three different counting sheets were provided for the interviewers with different selection ratios: 1:3, 1:5, and 1:10. The purpose of the counting sheets was to provide a means of counting the truck drivers entering the truck stop and to ensure that the selection of the truck drivers was random and not subject to interviewer choice. For each shift, one interviewer was assigned the job of counting and selecting the drivers. This interviewer selected a counting sheet with an appropriate sampling interval—1:10 for busy locations, 1:5 for average, or 1:3 for less busy locations.

As each adult entered the truck stop, the interviewer crossed off a number. If the number was highlighted, the person was approached and asked a series of screening questions to determine if the person was eligible for the study. If an eligible driver was found but the second interviewer was not available because they were already interviewing a driver, the driver was not selected for the study. The interviewer then resumed counting until a second highlighted number was reached. If the second interviewer was free and the person was eligible, an interview was attempted. It was assumed that the drivers selected but not interviewed because an interviewer was not available would be a random subset of the sample of truck drivers at a location.

Each shift was assigned one SRC interviewer and about five TIP interviewers. Each interviewer was expected to take about two interviews per three-hour time block and to work two of the three time blocks each day. There was always one interviewer doing the counting andtwo or three doing truck stop interviewing. Another interviewer did both counting and interviewing for the fuel line sample. The SRC interviewer's role was to coordinate the interviewing effort at each site and to do a limited amount of interviewing. The SRC interviewer was also responsible for checking interviews, answering questions, and sending information to the Control Office for sample management.

The use of truck parking spaces as a MOS appears to have worked well in practice. The final sampling report showed that there was a correspondence between the number of truck parking spaces and the volume of truck drivers entering a truck stop. However, because these measures of size were not equal, the sample could not be designed to be an equal probability or self-weighting sample. In order to compensate for the unequal probabilities of selection of truck drivers across the different sites, sampling weights should be used for descriptive analyses of the survey data. The construction of these weights is described in the following section.

Construction of Sampling Weights

The overall probability of selection for an individual truck driver is the product of the probabilities at each of the stages of selection. The first stage of selection is the PPS selection of the twenty truck stops. The probability that each truck stop was selected is 1955. Although 20 truck stops were selected, interviewing was actually conducted in only 19 of the 20 truck stops. The probability that each truck stop was selected is 19 times its MOS (number of truck parking spaces) divided by the total MOS of all of the truck stops in the five state sampling frame. For example, in this study, the total MOS was 38,038. The first-stage probability of selection of a truck stop with 250 truck parking spaces would be:

$$f_1 = (19 \times 250) \div 38,038 = 0.125.$$

The second stage of selection, the assignment of days of the week and three hour shifts to each selected truck stop, was done primarily to ensure that all times of the week were covered and that the assignment of shifts was randomized across the twenty selected truck stops. The original plan was to have an equal number of interviewing shifts at each truck stop. However, in practice, the number of shifts varied from four to eight with the largest number of truck stops conducting interviewing during six shifts.

The third stage sampling rate, the probability of selection of truck drivers during each shift, was estimated as the number of interviews conducted at a truck stop divided by the number of truck drivers counted by the interviewers during eight shifts. The number of truck

■ Table 2. Calculation of Weights for Long-form (Inside) Interviews

SITE NUMBER	MOS	WALK THROUGHS	ELIGIBILITY RATE	ADJUSTED WALK THROUGHS	INTERVIEWS	F_1	F_2	SAMPLING WEIGHT
1	75	739	0.500	739	27	0.037	0.073	369.9
3	175	947	0.659	1082	35	0.087	0.049	234.3
4	305	1641	0.701	1641	38	0.152	0.033	199.2
5	20	806	0.217	921	32	0.010	0.160	623.7
6	70	180	0.722	360	13	0.035	0.050	571.4
7	100	421	0.543	481	30	0.050	0.115	174.3
8	150	604	0.750	805	32	0.075	0.053	251.7
9	200	1208	0.234	1611	33	0.100	0.088	114.0
10	25	305	0.563	407	27	0.012	0.118	678.4
11	66	409	0.245	545	18	0.033	0.135	225.0
12	150	1306	0.844	1493	32	0.075	0.025	525.2
13	75	705	0.897	940	46	0.037	0.055	489.0
14	150	626	0.487	715	32	0.075	0.092	145.3
15	100	718	0.763	957	32	0.050	0.044	456.7
16	250	1256	0.482	1256	30	0.125	0.050	161.5
17	200	971	0.574	971	23	0.100	0.041	242.5
18	30	126	0.408	144	28	0.015	0.477	139.9
19	90	580	0.432	773	41	0.045	0.123	181.4
20	250	489	0.640	652	24	0.125	0.058	139.2

drivers was estimated by multiplying the eligibility rate of the persons sampled by the number of persons counted (walk throughs). In order to be eligible for the study, a person had to answer Yes to the following three questions: 1. Do you work as a truck driver? 2. Do you have a commercial driver's license? 3. Are you currently driving a truck?

If there were fewer than eight shifts at a truck stop, the number of "walk throughs" was standardized to eight shifts by multiplying the

■ Table 3. Calculation of Weights for Short-form (Fuel line) Interviews

SITE NUMBER	MOS	WALK THROUGHS	ELIGIBILITY RATE	ADJUSTED WALK THROUGHS	INTERVIEWS	F_1	F_2	SAMPLING WEIGHT
1	75	20	0.867	20	11	0.037	0.635	42.6
3	175	38	0.944	43	17	0.087	0.414	27.7
4	305	64	0.857	64	11	0.152	0.201	32.8
5	20	27	0.917	31	10	0.010	0.354	282.8
6	70	10	1.000	20	5	0.035	0.250	114.3
7	100	56	0.913	64	21	0.050	0.359	55.6
8	150	31	1.000	41	11	0.075	0.266	50.1
9	200	0	0.000	0	0	0.100	0.000	0.0
10	25	48	0.435	64	10	0.012	0.359	222.8
11	66	25	0.462	33	6	0.033	0.390	77.8
12	150	70	0.933	80	12	0.075	0.161	83.0
13	75	43	1.000	57	12	0.037	0.209	127.5
14	150	46	1.167	53	14	0.075	0.228	58.5
15	100	37	0.909	49	10	0.050	0.223	89.8
16	250	28	1.000	28	5	0.1 25	0.1 79	44.8
17	200	46	1.000	46	9	0.100	0.196	51.2
18	30	5	1.000	6	4	0.015	0.700	95.3
19	90	11	1.000	15	4	0.045	0.273	81.6
20	250	31	1.000	41	13	0.125	0.315	25.5

number by a factor of eight divided by the actual number of shifts. By using the number of interviews conducted in place of the number of eligible persons sampled as the numerator of the third stage rate, a nonresponse adjustment for the site is incorporated in the sampling weight. Table 2 shows the MOS, selection rates, and sampling weights for the nineteen sites. The weights ranged from a minimum of 114.0 to a maximum of 678.4 with a mean of 307.6 and a standard deviation of 177.3.

The following example from table 2 shows the calculation of a sampling weight for drivers selected at the New Lamont A/T Plaza in Bolingbrook, Illinois. This truck stop had 175 truck parking spaces. Therefore its first stage probability of selection is $(19 \times 175) \div 38{,}038 = 0.087$. There were seven shifts with a total of 947 "walk throughs." A sample of ninety-one of the persons walking through were selected and approached by the interviewers. Sixty of these were eligible truck drivers. Therefore the eligibility rate was $60 \div 91 = 0.659$, and it can be assumed that approximately 65.9 percent of the 947 persons who walked through the truck stop were eligible. If there had been eight instead of seven shifts, the number of walk throughs would have been increased by a factor of $8 \div 7$ or 1.143. The number of interviews conducted was thirty-five. Therefore the overall probability of selection for truck drivers at the New Lamont A/T Plaza is:

$$f = (0.087 \cdot 35) \div (1.143 \times 947 \times 0.659) = 0.00427.$$

The sampling weight, which is the inverse of the probability of selection, is $1 \div 0.00427 = 234.3$. Sampling weights for the short interviews conducted at the fuel lines were calculated in a similar way. These weights are shown in Table 3.

Text of the Full Survey

FOR OFFICE USE ONLY	**1997** University of Michigan Trucking Industry Project **Survey of Truck Drivers**

PROJECT: 790
(459155)
SUMMER/FALL 1997
Rev.: 7-24-97

The University of Michigan Survey Research Center Institute for Social Research Ann Arbor, MI 48106	1. INTERVIEWER LABEL

2. SAMPLE ID:

3. SITE NAME:

4. SITE NUMBER:

5. DATE:

6. LENGTH OF IW:

7. MODE: FTF   TELEPHONE

STATEMENT OF CONFIDENTIALITY MUST BE READ TO RESPONDENT:

Before we start, I would like to assure you that this interview is confidential and completely voluntary. If we should come to any question which you do not want to answer, just let me know, and we will go on to the next question.

FOR OFFICE USE ONLY			
DATE REC'D.	PROJECT STAFF REV.	DATE ENTERED	

TIME NOW:

A. WORK HISTORY

A1   Are you primarily an over the road or local pick-up and delivery driver?

| 1. OVER-THE-ROAD | 2. LOCAL PICK-UP AND DELIVERY |

A2   About how many miles did you drive your truck last year?

MILES

A3   About how many miles is your typical run or dispatch?

MILES

A4   What geographic region do you usually work in?
        [PROBE AO, ACCEPT MULTIPLE RESPONSES]   _____

        _____

A5   What city and state is your home base or domicile point?

        _____   _____
                                                              CITY   STATE

A6   How many years have you worked as a truck driver?

YEARS

A7   How old were you when you first worked as a commercial truck driver?

YEARS OLD

A8   You are currently a (RESPONSE A1) driver. Have you worked other jobs in the trucking
        industry?

| 1. YES | 5. NO | GO TO A10

A9   Have you ever worked as ...in the trucking industry as your primary job? [DO NOT READ CURRENT STATUS FROM A1]

	1. YES	5. NO
a. ...an over-the-road driver (IF NOT CURRENT)	1. YES	5. NO
b. ...a local delivery driver (IF NOT CURRENT)	1. YES	5. NO
c. ...a dock worker	1. YES	5. NO
d. ...a mechanic	1. YES	5. NO
e. ...a dispatcher	1. YES	5. NO
f. ...a hostler or yard worker	1. YES	5. NO
g. ...any other position in the trucking industry	1. YES	5. NO
h. SPECIFY:		

A10   Have you ever worked in an industry other than trucking?

    1. YES   5. NO   GO TO A13

A11   What industry was that?

_____

_____

A12   What job did you do in that industry?

_____

A13   To the nearest thousand dollars, how much did you earn in 1996 from your work as a truck driver?

               DOLLARS

A14   Have you been unemployed at any time in the last 12 months?

    1. YES   5. NO   GO TO A16

A15   How long were you unemployed in the last 12 months?

                        DAYS / WEEKS / MONTHS
                        [CIRCLE ONE]

A16   Have you been laid off from a driving job in the last 12 months because of lack of work, partial or complete closure of the terminal or a company going out of business ?

| 1. YES | 5. NO |

A17   Have you quit a driving job in the last 12 months?

| 1. YES | 5. NO |

A18   Have you been fired from a driving job in the last 12 months?

| 1. YES | 5. NO |

A19   Have you had an on-the-job injury that has kept you away from work for at least one day in the last twelve months?

| 1. YES | 5. NO |

A20   Have you received a worker's compensation payment in the last twelve months?

| 1. YES | 5. NO |

A21   Have you been away from work for a week or more because of illness in the last twelve months?

| 1. YES | 5. NO |

A22   In the last twelve months, have you been involved in an accident which was reported to the police while you were driving a truck or commercial vehicle?

| 1. YES | 5. NO |

A23   Have you been cited for a moving violation while on duty in the last twelve months?

| 1. YES | 5. NO |

B. INDUSTRY SEGMENT

We would like to know about the company or organization you work for. Remember, we <u>do</u> <u>not</u> want to know its name.

B1   How would you describe your employer ...

> [   ] READ
> else, but
> - ...for hire, a company whose primary business is trucking;
>   - ...private carriage, a company whose primary business is something which has some trucks, or
> - ...a government agency?

[1. FOR HIRE]   B2a   Please tell me what type of trucking company it is:
[RECORD VERBATIM]

_____

_____
                                                          GO TO B3

[2. PRIVATE CARRIAGE]   B2b   What industry are you employed by - for example, auto parts distribution, wholesale grocer, office furniture manufacturing, ...?

_____
                                                          GO TO B3

[3. GOVERNMENT]   B2c   Do you work for the federal, state, or local government?

[1. FEDERAL] [2. STATE] [3. LOCAL]

B3   What type of trailer are you pulling today? MARK ALL THAT APPLY, READ:

01 ____ dry box

02 ____ refrigerated

03 ____ tank

04 ____ flat bed

05 ____ drop deck

06 ____ autocarrrier

07 ____ container/intermodal

08 ____ bobtail (no trailer)

09 ____ other (specify)_____

B4   Are you driving alone, as part of a team, or as a trainer or trainee?

| 1. TEAM | 2. ALONE | 3. TRAINER/ TRAINEE |

⇓   GO TO SECTION C, PAGE 6

B5   When you are working in a team, how many hours of unbroken sleep do you typically get at a time?

| | HOURS

C. CHECKPOINT: EMPLOYEES / OWNER OPERATORS

C1　Are you an employee of a trucking firm, or are you an owner-operator?

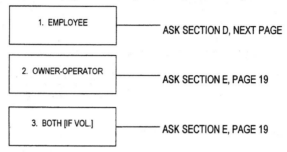

1. EMPLOYEE ——— ASK SECTION D, NEXT PAGE

2. OWNER-OPERATOR ——— ASK SECTION E, PAGE 19

3. BOTH [IF VOL.] ——— ASK SECTION E, PAGE 19

D. EMPLOYEES OF TRUCKING FIRMS

D1   Is this a year round, full-time, permanent job?

1. YES		5. NO
GO TO D3

D2   Is this job seasonal, part-time, temporary or casual? (CHECK ALL THAT APPLY).

1. SEASONAL		2. PART-TIME		3. TEMPORARY OR CASUAL

D3   How long have you worked for your current firm?   DAYS/
                                                                           MONTHS/ YEARS
                                                                 CIRCLE APPROPRIATE UNIT

        IF MORE THAN 1 YEAR WITH FIRM <u>AND</u> D1 IS YES, GO TO D12

D4   How many different carriers have you worked for
        in the last 12 months?   CARRIERS

D5 – D11 DO NOT EXIST FOR THIS QUESTIONNAIRE.

D12   How many drivers work for your company at all   DRIVERS
        locations ? PROBE: WHAT'S YOUR BEST ESTIMATE

        PROBE IF NECESSARY: Would you say it was ...

1. <25	2. 25-99	3. 100-249	4. 250-499	5. 500-999	6. >=1000

D13   About how many people does your company employ at
        all locations -- please include all employees, not only
        drivers but mechanics, sales workers, secretaries,
        and other employees? PROBE: WHAT'S YOUR BEST ESTIMATE]

                        EMPLOYEES

        PROBE IF NECESSARY: Would you say it was ...

1. <25	2. 25-99	3. 100-249	4. 250-499	5. 500-999	6. >=1000

			FOR EACH YES, ASK
D14	How are you being paid for your <u>driving</u> time on your current trip? Are you paid...		D15 Including pay for items such as multiple trailers and hazardous materials, what is your rate on this trip?
a.	....by the mile?	1. YES	5. NO GO TO D14b	a. $_____ PER MILE b. Is this the rate for a loaded truck? | 1. YES | | 5. NO | GO TO D15c GO TO D15d c. What is your empty rate? _____ PER MILE d. What is your loaded rate? _____ PER MILE
b.	....a percentage of revenue?	1. YES	5. NO GO TO D14c	_____ PERCENT
c.	...by the hour?	1. YES	5. NO GO TO D14d	_____ PER HOUR
d.	... some other way?	1. YES	5. NO GO TO D17	_____ PER _____
SPECIFY:			

D16 Are you currently…			D17 How much (additional / less) compensation do you receive for this? [IF NO DIFFERENCE IN COMPENSATION, ENTER 0]
a …pulling multiple trailers?	1. YES	5. NO	$_____ PER _____ ADDITIONAL/ LESS [CIRCLE ONE]
b … carrying hazardous materials?	1. YES	5. NO	$_____ PER _____ ADDITIONAL/ LESS [CIRCLE ONE]
c …deadheading (unloaded trailer)?	1. YES	5. NO	$_____ PER _____ ADDITIONAL/ LESS [CIRCLE ONE]

D18 Do you receive additional compensation for driving such as …		
a … extra payments for on-time performance?	1. YES	5. NO
b … a safety bonus?	1. YES	5. NO
c …other special payments? Specify:	1. YES	5. NO

D19 If you end up arriving late for a drop-off or pick-up will you…		
a …have your pay reduced?	1. YES	5. NO
b …lose work by missing a dispatch or getting a bad dispatch?	1. YES	5. NO
c …be disciplined with a warning or disciplinary suspension?	1. YES	5. NO
d …be penalized in some other way? Specify:	1. YES	5. NO
e I AM NOT PENALIZED FOR ARRIVING LATE [DO NOT READ]	1. YES	

I am interested in the last 24 hours you spent working - that is, from (CURRENT HOUR) yesterday to now. First, let's take driving time.

D20   How many miles have you driven since (CURRENT HOUR) yesterday?

                    MILES

D21   How many hours did you spend driving those miles?

                    HOURS

Still talking about the last 24 hours, let's turn to non-driving work time. I am interested in time spent on duty but not driving, including activities such as loading, unloading and drop and hook, as well as time spent waiting for things such as loading and unloading, getting into a dock, for dispatches or for bills to be cut. Please do not count meals or sleep time.

D22   How many hours have you spent on duty working, but not driving, in the last 24 hours?

                    HOURS

D23   How many hours have you slept in the last 24 hours?

                    HOURS   IF 0, GO TO D26

D24   Did you sleep in a motel, in a bunk in your truck, in your truck but not in a bunk, at home, or somewhere else? MARK ALL THAT APPLY.

1. IN A MOTEL	2. IN A BUNK IN THE TRUCK	3. IN THE TRUCK, NOT IN A BUNK	4. AT HOME

5. OTHER: SPECIFY

D25   About how much of your own money, not including expenses for which you will be reimbursed, have you spent on personal expenses such as motel rooms, meals, and personal long distance calls in the last 24 hours?

    $_____

Now I would like to ask about the last full trip or dispatch you completed, the dispatch before the one which brought you here. A full trip would start at the time you were dispatched and continue until you delivered your load to your final destination.

D26   Where did your last full trip begin (ORIGIN) ? _____

D27   What day and time did that trip begin?   _____ Day _____am/pm Time

D28   Where did that trip end (DESTINATION) ?   _____

D29   What day and time did that trip end?   _____ Day _____am/pm Time

D30   What kind of load did you carry on that trip?

_____

D31   Could you have loaded more if you were not limited by the weight of the load?

| 1. YES | | 5. NO |

D32   Could you have loaded more if you were not limited by the volume of the load?

| 1. YES | | 5. NO |

D33   About how many miles did you drive on that trip?

| | MILES

D33a   How many of those miles were driven with an empty trailer or with no trailer?

| | MILES

D34   About how many hours did you drive on that trip?

| | HOURS

D35   How many hours did you drive between 11:00pm and 7:00am?

| | HOURS WORKED AT NIGHT

D36   Did you have difficulty finding a place to park and take a rest on that trip?

| 1. YES | | 5. NO |

D37 – D38 DO NOT EXIST FOR THIS QUESTIONNAIRE.

a. On your trip from (origin) to (destination), how long did you have to wait for…?		b. Are you paid for…?		c. At what rate…?
D39	… a dispatch when away from your home or domicile point?	———— HOURS / MINUTES [CIRCLE ONE]	1. YES	5. NO GO TO D40	$_____ PER _____
D40	… loading/ unloading to begin or waiting while someone loaded or unloaded your truck?	———— HOURS / MINUTES [CIRCLE ONE]	1. YES	5. NO GO TO D41	$_____ PER _____
D41	….any other reasons?	———— HOURS / MINUTES [CIRCLE ONE]	1. YES	5. NO GO TO D42	$_____ PER _____
SPECIFY:				

a. On that trip, how much time did you spend…		b. Are you paid for…		c. At what rate…? ASK FOR EACH YES
D42 …. loading and unloading?	_____ HOURS / MINUTES [CIRCLE ONE]	1. YES	5. NO GO TO D43	$_____ PER _____
D43 ….dropping and hooking?	_____ HOURS / MINUTES [CIRCLE ONE]	1. YES	5. NO GO TO D44	$_____ PER _____
D44 …doing other work that I haven't mentioned?	_____ HOURS / MINUTES [CIRCLE ONE]	1. YES	5. NO GO TO D45	$_____ PER _____
Specify:				

D45   Which of the following best describes how you got your last load? READ SLOWLY

1.	You had complete control over what loads to consider and which one to take.

2.	You were able to pick your load, but you had some limitations, such as which loads you could pick.

3.	You were assigned your load, but you had some rights such as the right to refuse a load.

4.	You were assigned your load by your dispatcher.

D46   Did you use lumpers on your last trip?

1. YES	5. NO	7. N/A

                                        GO TO D48

D47   Does your company always, sometimes or never reimburse you when you use lumpers?

1. ALWAYS	2. SOMETIMES	3. NEVER

D48   What do you do when a dispatcher/shipper assigns an unrealistic delivery time?
        Do you... [READ ALL, MARK ALL THAT APPLY]

        a. _____ REFUSE THE LOAD
        b. _____ RENEGOTIATE THE TIME
        c. _____ DRIVE FASTER OR MORE HOURS
        d. _____ TAKE THE LOAD BUT DO NOT CHANGE YOUR DRIVING TIME OR SPEED
        e. _____ OTHER: _____

D49   Have you been asked to run overweight in the last month?

1. YES	5. NO

D50   Do you drive a regular route?

1. YES	5. NO

D51   Who decides the route you travel—does your dispatcher decide, do you decide, or do you
        decide with some suggestions from your dispatcher?

1. DISPATCHER DECIDES	2. YOU ROUTE YOURSELF	3. JOINTLY DECIDED

4. OTHER –SPECIFY: [IF VOL.]

D52   Returning to your trip from (origin) to (destination), was your route of that trip changed by
       you or by the company after you started that trip ?

       | 1. YES | | 5. NO | GO TO D54

D53   Why was your route changed? [READ ALL, MARK ALL THAT APPLY]

       01 _____ weather
       02 _____ traffic conditions
       03 _____ construction
       04 _____ new pick up or delivery
       05 _____ other. Specify: _____

D54   How many hours did you have off before your last trip?

       | _____ | NUMBER OF HOURS

D55   How many hours of sleep did you have during that time?

       | _____ | NUMBER OF HOURS   IF 0, GO TO D57

D56   Did you sleep in a motel, in a bunk in your truck, in your truck not in a bunk, at home or
       somewhere else? [READ ALL, MARK ALL THAT APPLY].

       | 1. IN A MOTEL | 2. IN A BUNK IN THE TRUCK | 3. IN THE TRUCK, NOT IN A BUNK | 4. AT HOME |

       | 5. OTHER: SPECIFY |

D57   When did you last spend at least 24 hours at home?

       | _____ | DAYS / WEEKS / MONTHS AGO
                             [CIRCLE ONE]

The next questions are about the work you have done in the last seven days –
that is, since last (DAY TODAY).

D58   How many days have you worked in the last seven days?

    [   ]   NUMBER OF DAYS

D59   How many dispatches have you had since last (DAY TODAY)?

    [   ]   NUMBER OF DISPATCHES

D60   About how many miles have you driven in the last seven days?

    [   ]   MILES

I am going to ask several questions about your last pay period. This is the period you worked to
earn your last paycheck.

D61   How much did you earn in your last pay period?
       (GROSS INCOME)

    [   ]   DOLLARS

D62   How long was that pay period?

    | 1. ONE WEEK | 2. TWO WEEKS | 3. ONE MONTH | 4. OTHER : |

D63   We are interested in comparing the hourly earnings of truck drivers with other employees,
       but it is difficult to get a good measure of the number of hours drivers work in a pay period.
       About how many hours did you spend on driving and non-driving work in your last pay
       period? It would be helpful if you could estimate how many hours you actually worked
       rather than the hours you logged.

    [   ]   HOURS

D64   Income can vary from pay period to pay period. When you are available to work a full pay
period ...

    a.   ...how much do you typically earn in a good (UNIT FROM D63)?

         $_____

    b.   ...how much do you typically earn in a slow (or bad) (UNIT FROM D63)?

         $_____

D65 – D66 DO NOT EXIST FOR THIS QUESTIONNAIRE.

I am going to ask you some questions about benefit plans such as pension plans and health
insurance.

a. Do you have (a)...			b. Is this through your... (record all that apply)	c. Does your company pay all, part, or none of the cost ...			d. Does your spouse have (his/her) own ...		
D67 ...deferred compensation plan such as a 401k, profit sharing, or stock purchase plan?	1. YES	5. NO GO TO D68	01. ___ COMPANY / UNION 05. ___ OTHER SPECIFY:	1. ALL	2. PART	3. NONE			
D68 ...conventional pension or retirement plan?	1. YES	5. NO GO TO D69	01. ___ COMPANY / UNION 02. ___ PRIVATE PURCHASE 03. ___ MILITARY 05. ___ OTHER SPECIFY:	1. ALL	2. PART	3. NONE	1. YES	5. NO	7. NA
D69 ... IRA (Individual Retirement Account)	1. YES	5. NO GO TO D70							
D70 ...health insurance?	1. YES	5. NO GO TO D71	01. ___ COMPANY / UNION 02. ___ SPOUSE 03. ___ PRIVATE PURCHASE 04. ___ MILITARY 05. ___ OTHER SPECIFY:	1. ALL	2. PART	3. NONE			

D71a.	D71b.
How many days of paid vacation does your employer provide annually?	How many days of paid and unpaid vacation did you take in the last 12 months?
_____	_____

D72a.	D72b.
How many paid sick days does your employer provide annually?	How many paid and unpaid sick days did you take in the last 12 months?
_____	_____

D73a.	D73b.
How many paid holidays does your employer provide annually?	Of those paid holidays, how many did you take off from work in the last 12 months?
_____	_____

GO TO SECTION G

E. QUESTIONS FOR OWNER-OPERATORS

E1   Is truck driving a year- round, full-time occupation for you?

1. YES		2. NO

Go To E2   E1a What, is your other occupation?

_____

E2   How long have you been an owner-operator?

	YEARS

E3   Do you have your own authority?

1. YES	5. NO

GO TO E4

E3a   How many years have you had operating authority? _____

E4   How many trucks do you own or lease?

	NUMBER

IF 1, GO TO E5a
IF 2 OR MORE, GO TO E5b

E5a   Do you own or lease your truck?

1. OWN	2. LEASE

GO TO E6   GO TO E7

E5b   Do you own or lease your trucks?

1. OWN ALL	2. LEASE ALL	3. BOTH

GO TO E6   GO TO E7   GO TO E6

E6　For the truck(s) you own, how did you finance the purchase — did you finance it … ?
MARK ALL THAT APPLY

1.　___ … yourself? (CHECK HERE IF R SAYS CASH)
2.　___ … through a bank or loan company?
3.　___ …through a truck dealer?
4.　___ …through the company you're leased to for hauling freight?
5.　___ …in some other way?

IF R LEASES TRUCK(S), (E5a or E5b = 2 or 3) ASK E7
OTHERS, GO TO E8

E7　For the truck(s) you lease, who holds the lease -- the company you drive for, a third-party firm, or someone else?

1. COMPANY	2. THIRD-PARTY	3. OTHER:

E8　Not including yourself, how many drivers do you employ?

DRIVERS

E9　Do you get most of your shipments from a permanent lease, through brokers, through a contract with shippers, or some other way?

1. PERMANENT LEASE	GO TO E10a

2. BROKERS	GO TO E10B

3. CONTRACT WITH SHIPPERS	GO TO E10c

4. OTHER: Explain	GO TO E15

E10a   How long have you been leased to your present carrier?

_____YEARS   GO TO E11

E10b   How many different freight brokers do you normally do business with in a month?

_____ # BROKERS   GO TO E14

E10c   How many different shippers do you typically do business with in a month

_____ # SHIPPERS   GO TO E14

E11   Does the company to which you are permanently leased provide complete maintenance for your truck, partial maintenance, or no maintenance at all?

1. COMPLETE	2. PARTIAL	3. NONE

E12   How many owner-operators work for the company you're permanently leased to?

OWNER OPERATORS

PROBE: What is your best estimate?

PROBE IF NECESSARY: Would you say it was ...

1. <25	2. 25-99	3. 100-249	4. 250-499	5. 500-999	6. >=1000

E13   How many company drivers does the firm you are permanently leased to employ?

HIRED DRIVERS

PROBE: What is your best estimate?

PROBE IF NECESSARY: Would you say it was ...

1. <25	2. 25-99	3. 100-249	4. 250-499	5. 500-999	6. >=1000

				FOR EACH YES, ASK
E14	How are you being paid for your <u>driving</u> time on your current trip? Are you paid…			E15 Including pay for items such as multiple trailers and hazardous materials, what is your rate on this trip?

a.	….by the mile?	1. YES	5. NO
			
			GO TO E14b
				a. $_____ PER MILE
				
				b. Is this the rate for a loaded truck?
				
				      | 1. YES | 5. NO |
				      GO TO D15c GO TO D15d
				
				c. What is your empty rate?
				  _____ PER MILE
				
				d. What is your loaded rate?
				  _____ PER MILE

b.	….a percentage of revenue?	1. YES	5. NO GO TO E14c	_____ PERCENT
c.	…by the hour?	1. YES	5. NO GO TO E14d	_____ PER HOUR
d.	… some other way?	1. YES	5. NO GO TO E14e	_____ PER ____

SPECIFY:

E16 Are you currently...			E17 How much (additional / less) compensation do you receive for this? [IF NO DIFFERENCE IN COMPENSATION, ENTER 0]
a	...pulling multiple trailers?	1. YES 5. NO	$_____ PER _____ ADDITIONAL/ LESS [CIRCLE ONE]
b	... carrying hazardous materials?	1. YES 5. NO	$_____ PER _____ ADDITIONAL/ LESS [CIRCLE ONE]
c	...deadheading (unloaded trailer)?	1. YES 5. NO	$_____ PER _____ ADDITIONAL/ LESS [CIRCLE ONE]

E18	Do you receive additional compensation for driving such as ...		
a	... extra payments for on-time performance?	1. YES	5. NO
b	... a safety bonus?	1. YES	5. NO
c	...other special payments? Specify:	1. YES	5. NO

E19	If you end up arriving late for a drop-off or pick-up will you...		
a	...have your pay reduced?	1. YES	5. NO
b	...lose work by missing a dispatch or getting a bad dispatch?	1. YES	5. NO
c	...be disciplined with a warning or disciplinary suspension?	1. YES	5. NO
d	...be penalized in some other way? Specify:	1. YES	5. NO
e	I AM NOT PENALIZED FOR ARRIVING LATE [DO NOT READ]	1. YES	

I am interested in the last 24 hours you spent working - that is from (CURRENT HOUR) yesterday to now. First, let's take driving time.

E20   How many miles have you driven since (CURRENT HOUR) yesterday?

┌─────────────┐
│   │   MILES
└─────────────┘

E21   How many hours did you spend driving those miles?

┌─────────────┐
│   │   HOURS
└─────────────┘

Still talking about the last 24 hours, let's turn to non-driving work time. I am interested in time spent on-duty but not driving. This includes activities such as loading, unloading and drop and hook, as well as time spent waiting for things such as loading and unloading, getting into a dock, for dispatches or for bills to be cut. Please do not count meals or sleep time.

E22   How many hours have you spent on duty working but not driving in the last 24 hours?

┌─────────────┐
│   │   HOURS
└─────────────┘

E23   How many hours have you slept in the last 24 hours?

┌─────────────┐
│   │   HOURS   IF 0, GO TO E26
└─────────────┘

E24   Did you sleep in a motel, in a bunk in your truck, in your truck but not in a bunk, at home, or somewhere else? MARK ALL THAT APPLY.

1. IN A MOTEL	2. IN A BUNK IN THE TRUCK	3. IN THE TRUCK, NOT IN A BUNK	4. AT HOME

5. OTHER: SPECIFY

E25   About how much of your own money, not including expenses for which you will be reimbursed, have you spent on personal expenses such as motel rooms, meals, and personal long distance calls in the last 24 hours?

        $_____

Now I would like to ask about the last full trip or dispatch you completed, the dispatch before the one which brought you here. A full trip would start at the time you were dispatched and continue until you delivered your load to your final destination.

E26   Where did your last full trip begin (ORIGIN) ? _____

E27   What day and time did that trip begin?   _____ Day _____am/pm Time

E28   Where did that trip end (DESTINATION) ?   _____

E29   What day and time did that trip end?   _____ Day _____am/pm Time

E30   What kind of load did you carry on that trip?

        _____

E31   Could you have loaded more if you were not limited by the weight of the load?

        | 1. YES | | 5. NO |

E32   Could you have loaded more if you were not limited by the volume of the load?

        | 1. YES | | 5. NO |

E33   How many hours did the trip from (ORIGIN) to (DESTINATION) take?
        IF 1 OR 2 DAYS, PROBE FOR HOURS

        | | HOURS | | DAYS

E34   About how many miles did you drive on that trip?

        | | MILES

E34a   How many of those miles were driven with an empty trailer or with no trailer?

        | | MILES

E35   About how many hours did you drive on that trip?

        | | HOURS

E36   How many hours did you work between 11:00pm and 7:00am?

        | |

E37   Now remembering how we defined on-duty non-driving time, how many hours of non-driving work did you do on the trip from (ORIGIN) to (DESTINATION)?

[_____] HOURS

E38   Did you have difficulty finding a place to park and take a rest on that trip?

[1. YES]   [5. NO]

a.	On your trip from (origin) to (destination), how long did you have to wait for...?	b. Are you paid for...?		c. At what rate...?
E39	... a dispatch when away from your home or domicile point?	———— HOURS / MINUTES [CIRCLE ONE]	1. YES	5. NO GO TO E40	$_____ PER _____
E40	... loading/ unloading to begin or waiting while someone loaded or unloaded your truck?	———— HOURS / MINUTES [CIRCLE ONE]	1. YES	5. NO GO TO E41	$_____ PER _____
E41	....any other reasons?	———— HOURS / MINUTES [CIRCLE ONE]	1. YES	5. NO GO TO E42	$_____ PER _____
SPECIFY:				

a. On that trip, how much time did you spend...	b. Are you paid for...		c. At what rate...? ASK FOR EACH YES
E42 .... loading and unloading? HOURS / MINUTES [CIRCLE ONE]	1. YES	5. NO GO TO E43	$_____ PER _____
E43 ....dropping and hooking? HOURS / MINUTES [CIRCLE ONE]	1. YES	5. NO GO TO E44	$_____ PER _____
E44 ...doing other work that I haven't mentioned? HOURS / MINUTES [CIRCLE ONE]	1. YES	5. NO GO TO E45	$_____ PER _____

Specify:

E45   Which of the following best describes how you got your last load? READ SLOWLY

1.	You had complete control over what loads to consider and which one to take.

2.	You were able to pick your load, but you had some limitations, such as which loads you could pick.

3.	You were assigned your load, but you had some rights such as the right to refuse a load.

4.	You were assigned your load by your dispatcher.

E46 Did you use lumpers on your last trip?

1. YES	5. NO	7. N/A

GO TO E48

E47 Does your company always, sometimes or never reimburse you when you use lumpers?

1. ALWAYS	2. SOMETIMES	3. NEVER

E48 What do you do when a dispatcher/shipper assigns an unrealistic delivery time?
Do you... [READ ALL, MARK ALL THAT APPLY]

a. _____ REFUSE THE LOAD
b. _____ RENEGOTIATE THE TIME
c. _____ DRIVE FASTER OR MORE HOURS
d. _____ TAKE THE LOAD BUT DO NOT CHANGE YOUR DRIVING TIME OR SPEED
e. _____ OTHER: _____

E49 Have you been asked to run overweight in the last month?

1. YES	5. NO

E50 Do you drive a regular route?

1. YES	5. NO

E51 Who decides the route you travel—does the shipper/dispatcher decide, do you decide, or do you decide with some suggestions from your shipper/dispatcher?

1. SHIPPER/ DISPATCHERDECIDES	2. YOU ROUTE YOURSELF	3. DECIDE JOINTLY

4. OTHER –SPECIFY: [IF VOL.]

E52   Was the route of your last trip, from (origin) to (destination) changed after you started that trip ?

| 1. YES | 5. NO | GO TO E54
|---|---|

E53   Why was your route changed? [READ ALL, MARK ALL THAT APPLY]

01 _____ weather
02 _____ traffic conditions
03 _____ construction
04 _____ new customers
05 _____ other. Specify: _____

E54   How many hours did you have off between your last trip and this trip?

| | NUMBER OF HOURS
|---|

E55   How many hours of sleep did you have during that time?

| | NUMBER OF HOURS   IF 0, GO TO E57
|---|

E56   Did you sleep in a motel, in a bunk in your truck, in your truck not in a bunk, at home or somewhere else ...?   [READ ALL, MARK ALL THAT APPLY].

1. IN A MOTEL	2. IN A BUNK IN THE TRUCK	3. IN THE TRUCK, NOT IN A BUNK	4. AT HOME

5. OTHER: SPECIFY

E57   When did you last spend at least 24 hours at home?

| | DAYS / WEEKS / MONTHS AGO
|---| [CIRCLE ONE]

The next questions are about the work you have done in the last seven days - that is, since last (DAY TODAY).

E58   How many days have you worked in the last seven days?

        ┌──────────────┐
        │   │   NUMBER OF DAYS
        └──────────────┘

E59   How many dispatches have you had since last (DAY TODAY)?

        ┌──────────────┐
        │   │   NUMBER OF DISPATCHES
        └──────────────┘

E60   About how many miles have you driven in the last seven days?

        ┌──────────────┐
        │   │   MILES
        └──────────────┘

Now I am going to ask you several questions about the revenues you have earned in the last week.

E61   How much revenue have you earned from trucking in the last week?

        ┌──────────────┐
        │   │   DOLLARS
        └──────────────┘

E62   ASK ONLY IF R OWNS OR LEASES MULTIPLE TRUCKS (E4=2 OR MORE)
        Was this revenue from your own work and truck, or does it include other trucks that you own or lease?

        ┌──────────────┐   ┌──────────────┐
        │ 1. MY OWN   │   │ 5. MULTIPLE │
        │   TRUCK   │   │   TRUCKS   │
        └──────────────┘   └──────────────┘

E63   We are interested in comparing the hourly earnings of truck drivers with other employees. About how many hours did you spend on driving and non-driving work in the last week? It would be helpful if you could estimate how many hours you actually worked rather than the hours you logged.

        ┌──────────────┐
        │   │   HOURS
        └──────────────┘

E64   Income can vary from week to week. When you are available to work a full week ...

a.   ...how much do you typically earn in a good week? _____

b.   ...how much do you typically earn in a slow (or bad) week? _____

E65   Are you paid by the company leased to, a broker, the shipper, or by someone else?

1. COMPANY LEASED TO	2. BROKER	3. SHIPPER	4. OTHER (SPECIFY)

E66   How many days does it usually take from the time you complete a job until the time you get paid?

	DAYS

I am going to ask you some questions about benefit plans such as pension plans and health insurance.

a. Do you have (a)...			b. Is this through your... (record all that apply)	c. Does your company pay all, part, or none of the cost ...			d. Does your spouse have (his/her) own ...		
E67 ...deferred compensation plan such as a 401k, profit sharing, or stock purchase plan?	1. YES	5. NO GO TO E68	01. ___ COMPANY / UNION 05. ___ OTHER SPECIFY:	1. ALL	2. PART	3. NONE			
E68 ...conventional pension or retirement plan?	1. YES	5. NO GO TO E69	01. ___ COMPANY / UNION 02. ___ PRIVATE PURCHASE 03. ___ MILITARY 05. ___ OTHER SPECIFY:	1. ALL	2. PART	3. NONE	1. YES	5. NO	7. NA
E69 ... IRA (Individual Retirement Account)	1. YES	5. NO GO TO E70							
E70 ...health insurance?	1. YES	5. NO GO TO E71	01. ___ COMPANY / UNION 02. ___ SPOUSE 03. ___ PRIVATE PURCHASE 04. ___ MILITARY 05. ___ OTHER SPECIFY:	1. ALL	2. PART	3. NONE			

E71a.	E71b.
How many days of paid vacation does your employer provide annually?	How many days of paid and unpaid vacation did you take in the last 12 months?
_____	_____

E72a.	E72b.
How many paid sick days does your employer provide annually?	How many paid and unpaid sick days did you take in the last 12 months?
_____	_____

E73a.	E73b.
How many paid holidays does your employer provide annually?	Of those paid holidays, how many did you take off from work in the last 12 months?
_____	_____

E74   To the nearest thousand dollars, what was your annual gross revenue from trucking last year- - please include all trucks?

    [   ] DOLLARS

E75 To the nearest thousand dollars, how much did you earn last year in net after paying truck expenses, including any interest on loans on the truck(s)?

	DOLLARS

E76 At your current rates, would you take on more work if it were easily available?

| 5. NO | | 1. YES |

We are interested in why people choose to become owner-operators. I am going to read a list of reasons that some people give for choosing to become owner operators. Please rate each reason on a scale from 1 to 5 where 1 means not at all important and 5 means very important.

E77
How important was … in deciding to become an owner-operator?

a	…wanting to be independent	1 NOT AT ALL IMPORTANT	2	3	4	5 VERY IMPORTANT
b	…making more money	1 NOT AT ALL IMPORTANT	2	3	4	5 VERY IMPORTANT
c	…feeling that it was the only way to get a job in the industry	1 NOT AT ALL IMPORTANT	2	3	4	5 VERY IMPORTANT
d	…having more flexible hours and better working conditions	1 NOT AT ALL IMPORTANT	2	3	4	5 VERY IMPORTANT
e	….wanting to grow a business	1 NOT AT ALL IMPORTANT	2	3	4	5 VERY IMPORTANT

Were there other reasons you became an owner-operator?
[PROBE AO]

F. TECHNOLOGY

F1 Advanced communications technologies are rapidly becoming part of the trucking industry. Which of the following forms of communication do you use in your work as a driver?				F2 How many times have you used ...in the last 24 hours?	F3 Do you use this to communicate with your dispatcher?	
A...pay phone ?	1. YES	5. NO	9. DK		1. YES	5. NO
b...fax ? (1)	1. YES	5. NO	9. DK		1. YES	5. NO
c...beeper/message pager ? (2)	1. YES	5. NO	9. DK		1. YES	5. NO
d...2 way radio (not CB)? (3)	1. YES	5. NO	9. DK		1. YES	5. NO
e...cellular phone? (5)	1. YES	5. NO	9. DK		1. YES	5. NO
f...e-mail / Internet? (10)	1. YES	5. NO	9. DK		1. YES	5. NO
F4. Which of the following devices do you have in the truck you are driving today?				F5 How many times have you used ...in the last 24 hours?	F6 Do you use this to communicate with your dispatcher?	
A....personal computer such as a laptop or notebook? (6)	1. YES	5. NO	9. DK		1. YES	5. NO
b... scan bar code reader? (7)	1. YES	5. NO	9. DK		1. YES	5. NO
c... automatic vehicle location? (8)	1. YES	5. NO	9. DK		1. YES	5. NO
d... satellite-based system? (9)	1. YES	5. NO	9. DK		1. YES	5. NO
e... mobile fax? (11)	1. YES	5. NO	9. DK		1. YES	5. NO

IF ALL NO, GO TO F9
ELSE, FILL IN WORD FOR HIGHEST NUMBERED "YES" IN GRID

F7   What do you like about your (GADGET)? CHECK ALL THAT APPLY

_____

_____

DO NOT READ.

01 _____ I FEEL SAFER
02 _____ I DO MY JOB BETTER
03 _____ IT IS EASIER TO COMMUNICATE WITH MY FAMILY
04 _____ I CAN REACH MY FAMILY
05 _____ I DON'T HAVE TO STOP TO COMMUNICATE WITH MY DISPATCHER
06 _____ OTHER (PLEASE SPECIFY: _____)

F8   What don't you like about your (GADGET)? CHECK ALL THAT APPLY

_____

_____

DO NOT READ.

01 _____ I FEEL MONITORED
02 _____ IT CAN BE UNRELIABLE
03 _____ I RECEIVE OR PROVIDE TOO MUCH INFORMATION
04 _____ IT IS DIFFICULT TO USE
05 _____ OTHER (PLEASE SPECIFY: _____)

F9 Which of the following aids do you use for routing?			F10 About how many times in the last 24 hours have you used...	F11 What month and year did you first start using ...?
a ... road atlas/paper maps?	1. YES	5. NO		
b ... dispatcher?	1. YES	5. NO		
c ... CB to another driver?	1. YES	5. NO		
c ... cell phone?	1. YES	5. NO		_____MONTH 19 ___
e ... onboard computers displaying text and/or maps?	1. YES	5. NO		_____MONTH 19 ___
f ... personal computers with map systems and/or the Internet?	1. YES	5. NO		_____MONTH 19 ___
h ...some other routing aid? (SPECIFY)	1. YES	5. NO		_____MONTH 19 ___

F12   How does your company identify the location of your vehicle now?
DO NOT READ, MARK ALL THAT APPLY [PROBE AO']

_____

_____

1 _____ I CALL THE OFFICE WHEN I REACH TRUCK STOPS
2 _____ I CALL THE OFFICE ON MY CELLULAR PHONE
3 _____ AVL
4 _____ SATELLITE-BASED SYSTEM
5 _____ I DON'T KNOW
6 _____ OTHER. (PLEASE SPECIFY: _____)

G.   DEMOGRAPHICS

G1   RECORD GENDER BY OBSERVATION:

1. MALE	2. FEMALE

G2   How old are you?

YEARS OLD

G3   Are you currently married, widowed, divorced, separated or have you never been married?

1. MARRIED	2. WIDOWED	3. DIVORCED	4. SEPARATED	5. NEVER MARRIED
GO TO G4	GO TO G6	GO TO G5	GO TO G5	

GO TO G6

G4   Does your spouse work for pay full-time, part-time, or not at all?

1.FULL-TIME	2. PART-TIME	3. DOES NOT WORK

G5   Did you separate or divorce after becoming a truck driver?

1. YES	5. NO

G6   How many financially dependent children do you have?

DEPENDENT CHILDREN

G7   About what was your total family income last year?

$_____   GO TO G8

PROBE IF NECESSARY:
    G7a   Was it more or less than $30,000.00?

1. MORE	2. LESS

GO TO G7c

    G7b   Was it more than $45,000.00?

1. YES	5. NO

GO TO G8   GO TO G8

    G7c   Was it less than $20,000.00?

1. YES	5. NO

G8   Are you a military veteran?

1. YES	5. NO

G9   Do you consider yourself white, African American, Asian-American, Native American, or something else?

1. WHITE	2. AFRICAN AMERICAN	3. ASIAN-AMERICAN

4. NATIVE AMERICAN	5. OTHER

G10   Do you consider yourself to be Hispanic?

1. YES	5. NO

G11   What is the highest grade of school or year of college that you completed?
    PROMPT IF NECESSARY ; FILL IN CONTINUOUS NUMBER IF GIVEN.

01. LESS THAN HIGH SCHOOL (8th GRADE OR LESS)	04. VOCATIONAL OR TECHNICAL SCHOOL	07. COLLEGE OR GRADUATE DEGREE
02. SOME HIGH SCHOOL (9th - 12th GRADE)	05. SOME COLLEGE (NO DEGREE)	
03. HIGH SCHOOL DEGREE	06. ASSOCIATE DEGREE	GRADE/YEAR

G12 How did you learn to drive commercial trucks? Did you learn in a program given by a private technical college, a course given by a public technical or community college, in the military, through a program provided by a trucking company or did you pick it up on the job?

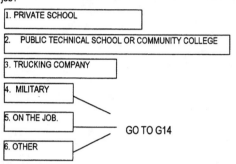

1. PRIVATE SCHOOL

2. PUBLIC TECHNICAL SCHOOL OR COMMUNITY COLLEGE

3. TRUCKING COMPANY

4. MILITARY

5. ON THE JOB. ⎯⎯⎯ GO TO G14

6. OTHER

G13 In what year did you complete that training program?

1. YEAR 19___	5. STILL ENROLLED [IF VOL.]	7. DID NOT COMPLETE [IF VOL.]

G14 Do you currently belong to a union?

1. YES	5. NO
	GO TO G16

G15 What union do you belong to?

1. TEAMSTERS	2. OTHER:

GO TO SECTION H

G16 Have you ever been a member of a union?

1. YES	5. NO

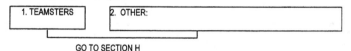

H. HOURS OF SERVICE AND LOG BOOKS

First, I would like to discuss your views of the federal regulations of hours of work.

H1   Do you keep a log book?

| 1. YES | 5. NO |

H2   In general, do you think log books accurately reflect the hours worked by most drivers?

| 1. YES | 5. NO |

H3   In the last 30 days, have you ever worked more hours than you recorded in your log book?

| 1. YES | 5. NO |

H4   In the last 30 days, about how many times have you ended up driving more than 10 hours without an eight hour break?

| |

H5 When you do drive more than 10 hours, is it often, sometimes, or never because (of)...	1. OFTEN	2. SOMETIMES	3. NEVER
a. ...you're on a tight schedule?			
b. ... weather conditions?			
c. ... traffic congestion or delays?			
d. ...you need to make more money?			
e. ...delays associated with dispatching?			
f. ...delays associated with loading/unloading?			
g. ...some other reason?			
SPECIFY:			

H6   How often have you found yourself dozing or falling asleep at the wheel in the last 30 days? [DO NOT READ]

| 1. NEVER | 2. ONCE | 3. TWICE | 4. 3 OR 4 TIMES |

| 5. MORE THAN 4 TIMES | 8. DON'T KNOW | 9. REFUSE TO ANSWER |

H7   What are the most common reasons drivers violate hours of service regulations? RECORD VERBATIM AND MARK ANY THAT APPLY.

_____

_____

     a. ____ WITHIN A SHORT DISTANCE OF DESTINATION WHEN HOURS RUN OUT
     b. ____ SHIPPERS SET UNREALISTIC REQUIREMENTS ON DELIVERIES
     c. ____ DELAYS IN LOADING/UNLOADING

H8   What changes in regulations would most improve drivers' work life?

_____

_____

_____

H9   What do you like most about current log book regulations?

_____

_____

_____

H10   What do you like least about current log book regulations?

_____

_____

_____

J. UNIONS AND RELATIONS WITH COMPANY

J1.   Now I would like you to evaluate your company's attitudes toward your needs. I am going
to read a list and for each issue, I would like you to tell me whether your company is very
concerned, somewhat concerned, or not at all concerned about that issue.

What is your company's attitude toward your need for ..... Would you say that your company is very concerned, somewhat concerned, or not at all concerned?	01 VERY CONCERNED	02 SOMEWHAT CONCERNED	03 NOT AT ALL CONCERNED
a ... improving your income			
b ...fringe benefits			
c ...time at home and well-being of family members			
d ...safety, quality and maintenance of equipment			
e ...not wasting your time			
f ...an accurate paycheck			
g ...safe working conditions and proper rest			
h ...protecting your health			
I ...having a secure and stable job			

J2   I would also like to ask your views on what would happen if more truck drivers became union members and the union played a larger role in the trucking industry.

I am going to read through a series of statements and you should let me know if you strongly agree, agree, disagree or strongly disagree.

If more truck drivers became union members and the union played are larger role in the industry ....

		01 STRONGLY AGREE	02 AGREE	03 DISAGREE	04 STRONGLY DISAGREE	[IF VOL.] DON'T KNOW
a	...drivers' earnings would increase.					
b	...there would be more conflict between employees and employers.					
c	...more drivers would get good health insurance and pensions.					
d	...employees would work fewer hours per week.					
e	...there would be strikes.					
f	...nothing would change but union officials would get rich.					
g	...the job would be safer.					
h	...drivers would be better off if the union were stronger.					

IF R IS UNION MEMBER (J14=YES), SKIP TO SECTION K (NEXT PAGE)

J3   If you had the opportunity to start working for a trucking company that employs union drivers, would you... [READ BOTH OPTIONS]

1. ...continue working for your current company, or

2. ...go to work for the unionized company?

3. DON'T KNOW [IF VOL.]

K. CLOSE OUT

To this point, most of our questions have been about the facts of being a truck driver. Now we would like to throw this open a bit and ask you for a few opinions.

K1   What do you enjoy most about your work?

_____

_____

_____

K2   What is most challenging about your work?

_____

_____

_____

K3   What do you enjoy least about your work?

_____

_____

_____

K4   a.   Would you like to be working as a truck driver in five years?

1. YES	5. NO

GO TO K5

b.   (Would you like to be working as a truck driver) in ten years?

1. YES	5. NO

K5   Do you feel that this is a career job, one you can keep doing until you retire?

_____

_____

_____

K6   No one has ever done a 'scientific' survey of what drivers enjoy listening to while they drive. Could you tell me the three types of programming you listen to most frequently beginning with your favorite?

1. _____

2. _____

3. _____

K7   Is there anything else you would like us to know about truck driving?

_____

_____

_____

We appreciate your time and wish you the best of luck with your work. I am going to give you my card so that you can contact me if you have any questions or want a copy of the report we produce from this survey. It will be about nine months before it is available.

RECORD TIME NOW:

THUMBNAIL SKETCH

Text of the Five-Minute Survey

FOR OFFICE USE ONLY	**1997** University of Michigan Trucking Industry Project **Survey of Truck Drivers** -SHORT FORM-

PROJECT: 790
(459155)
SUMMER/FALL 1997
Rev.: 7-24-97

The University of Michigan Survey Research Center Institute for Social Research Ann Arbor, MI 48106	1. INTERVIEWER LABEL

2. SAMPLE ID:

3. SITE NAME:

4. SITE NUMBER:

5. DATE:

6. LENGTH OF IW:

7. MODE: FTF   TELEPHONE

STATEMENT OF CONFIDENTIALITY MUST BE READ TO RESPONDENT:

Before we start, I would like to assure you that this interview is confidential and completely voluntary. If we should come to any question which you do not want to answer, just let me know, and we will go on to the next question.

A. WORK HISTORY

A1   Are you primarily an over-the-road or local pick-up and delivery driver?

1. OVER-THE-ROAD	2. LOCAL PICK-UP AND DELIVERY

A2   About how many miles did you drive your truck last year?

MILES

A3   About how many miles is your typical run or dispatch?

MILES

A4   What geographic region do you usually work in?
[PROBE AO, ACCEPT MULTIPLE RESPONSES]

A5   What city and state is your home base or domicile point?

CITY   STATE

A6   How many years have you worked as a truck driver?

YEARS

A7   To the nearest thousand dollars, how much did you earn last year from your work as a truck driver?

DOLLARS

A8   In the last twelve months, have you been involved in an accident which was reported to the police while you were driving a truck or commercial vehicle?

1. YES	5. NO

A9   Have you been cited for a moving violation while on duty in the last twelve months?

1. YES	5. NO

B. INDUSTRY SEGMENT

We would like to know about the company or organization you work for. Remember, we <u>do</u> <u>not</u> want to know its name.

B1   How would you describe your employer ...

[READ]
- ...for hire, a company whose primary business is trucking;
- ...private carriage, a company whose primary business is something else, but which has some trucks, or
- ...a government agency?

1. FOR HIRE

B2a   Please tell me what type of trucking company it is:
[RECORD VERBATIM]

_____

_____

GO TO B3

2. PRIVATE CARRIAGE

B2b   What industry are you employed by - for example, auto parts distribution, wholesale grocer, office furniture manufacturing, ...?

_____

GO TO B3

3. GOVERNMENT

B2c   Do you work for the federal, state, or local government?

| 1. FEDERAL | 2. STATE | 3. LOCAL |

B3   Are you driving alone, as part of a team, or as a trainer or trainee?

| 1. TEAM | 2. ALONE | 3. TRAINER/ TRAINEE |

C1. CHECKPOINT: Are you an employee of a trucking firm, or are you an owner-operator?

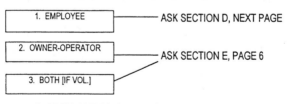

1. EMPLOYEE ——— ASK SECTION D, NEXT PAGE

2. OWNER-OPERATOR ——— ASK SECTION E, PAGE 6

3. BOTH [IF VOL.]

D. EMPLOYEES OF TRUCKING FIRMS:

D1   Is this a year round, full-time, permanent job?

| 1. YES | | 5. NO |

D2   How long have you worked for your current firm?

| | DAYS/MONTHS/ YEARS

CIRCLE UNIT

D3   About how many people does your company employ at
all locations -- please include all employees, not only
drivers but mechanics, sales workers, secretaries, and other employees?
PROBE: What's your best estimate?

| | EMPLOYEES

PROBE IF NECESSARY: Would you say it was ...

| 1. <25 | 2. 25-99 | 3. 100-249 | 4. 250-499 | 5. 500-999 | 6. >=1000 |

The next questions are about the way that you are paid for your work.

				FOR EACH YES, ASK
D4	How are you being paid for your <u>driving</u> time on your current trip? Are you paid...			**D5** Including pay for items such as multiple trailers and hazardous materials, what is your rate on this trip?
a.	....by the mile?	1. YES	5. NO GO TO D4b	a. $_____ PER MILE b. Is this the rate for a loaded truck? 　1. YES　　　　5. NO GO TO D5c　　GO TO D5d c. What is your empty rate? _____ PER MILE d. What is your loaded rate? _____ PER MILE
b.	....a percentage of revenue?	1. YES	5. NO GO TO D4c	_____ PERCENT
c.	...by the hour?	1. YES	5. NO GO TO D4d	_____ PER HOUR
d.	... some other way?	1. YES	5. NO GO TO D6	_____ PER _____
SPECIFY:				

I'm interested in your work in the last 24 hour period, that is from (CURRENT HOUR) yesterday to now.

D6   How many miles have you driven since (CURRENT HOUR) yesterday?

        ┌─────────┐
        │   │ MILES
        └─────────┘

D7   How many hours did you spend driving those miles?

        ┌─────────┐
        │   │ HOURS
        └─────────┘

Still talking about the last 24 hours, let's turn to non-driving work time. I am interested in time spent on duty but not driving, including activities such as loading, unloading and drop and hook, as well as time spent waiting for things such as loading and unloading, getting into a dock, for dispatches or for bills to be cut. Please do not count meals or sleep time.

D8   How many hours have you spent on duty working, but not driving, in the last 24 hours?

        ┌─────────┐
        │   │ HOURS
        └─────────┘

D9   How many hours have you slept in the last 24 hours?

        ┌─────────┐
        │   │ HOURS
        └─────────┘

Now I am going to ask you some questions about some benefit plans you may have.

D10 Do you have a...			D11 Is this through your...
A ...pension or retirement plan?	1. YES	5. NO	01. ___ COMPANY OR UNION 02. ___ PRIVATE PURCHASE 03. ___ MILITARY 04. ___ OTHER:
B...health insurance?	1. YES	5. NO	01. ___ COMPANY OR UNION 02. ___ SPOUSE 02. ___ PRIVATE PURCHASE 03. ___ MILITARY 04. ___ OTHER:

GO TO SECTION F, PAGE 9

E. QUESTIONS FOR OWNER-OPERATORS:

E1   How long have you been an owner-operator?

```
┌──────────────┐
│              │   YEARS
└──────────────┘
```

E2   Do you own or lease your truck?

| 1. OWN | 2. LEASE | 3. BOTH |

E3   Do you get most of your shipments from permanent lease, through brokers, or some other way?

```
┌────────────────────┐
│ 1. PERMANENT LEASE  │
└────────────────────┘

    ┌────────────────┐
    │ 2. BROKERS     │
    └────────────────┘
                             SKIP TO E7
┌──────────────────┐
│ 3. OTHER WAY     │
└──────────────────┘
```

E4   How many owner-operators work for the company you're permanently leased to?

```
┌──────────────┐
│              │   OWNER OPERATORS
└──────────────┘
```

PROBE: What is your best estimate?

PROBE IF NECESSARY: Would you say it was ...

| 1. <25 | 2. 25-99 | 3. 100-249 | 4. 250-499 | 5. 500-999 | 6. >=1000 |

E5   How many company drivers does the firm you are permanently leased to employ?

```
┌──────────────┐
│              │   HIRED DRIVERS
└──────────────┘
```

PROBE: What is your best estimate?

PROBE IF NECESSARY: Would you say it was ...

| 1. <25 | 2. 25-99 | 3. 100-249 | 4. 250-499 | 5. 500-999 | 6. >=1000 |

E6   How long have you been working with this company?

```
┌──────────────┐
│              │   YEARS / MONTHS
└──────────────┘
```

The next questions are about the way that you are paid for your work.

		FOR EACH YES, ASK
E7	How are you being paid for your <u>driving</u> time on your current trip? Are you paid…	E8 Including pay for items such as multiple trailers and hazardous materials, what is your rate on this trip?
a.	….by the mile?	1. YES / 5. NO GO TO E7b	a. $_____ PER MILE b. Is this the rate for a loaded truck? 1. YES | 5. NO GO TO E8c | GO TO E8d c. What is your empty rate? _____ PER MILE d. What is your loaded rate? _____ PER MILE
b.	….a percentage of revenue?	1. YES / 5. NO GO TO E7c	_____ PERCENT
c.	…by the hour?	1. YES / 5. NO GO TO E7d	_____ PER HOUR
d.	… some other way?	1. YES / 5. NO GO TO E9	_____ PER _____
SPECIFY:			

I am interested in the last 24 hours you spent working - that is from (CURRENT HOUR) yesterday to now. First, let's take driving time.

E9   How many miles have you driven since (CURRENT HOUR) yesterday?

    ☐ MILES

E10   How many hours did you spend driving those miles?

    ☐ HOURS

Still talking about the last 24 hours, let's turn to non-driving work time. I am interested in time spent <u>on-duty but not driving</u>. This includes activities such as loading, unloading and drop and hook, as well as time spent waiting for things such as loading and unloading, getting into a dock, for dispatches or for bills to be cut. Please do not count meals or sleep time.

E11   How many hours have you spent on duty working but not driving in the last 24 hours?

    ☐ HOURS

E12   How many hours have you slept in the last 24 hours?

    ☐ HOURS

Now I am going to ask you some questions about some benefit plans you may have.

E13 Do you have a…			E14 Is this through your…
A…pension or retirement plan?	1. YES	5. NO	01. ___ COMPANY OR UNION 02. ___ PRIVATE PURCHASE 03. ___ MILITARY 04. ___ OTHER:
B…health insurance?	1. YES	5. NO	01. ___ COMPANY OR UNION 02. ___ PRIVATE PURCHASE 03. ___ MILITARY 04. ___ OTHER:
C…an IRA or Keogh plan?	1. YES	5. NO	01. ___ COMPANY OR UNION 02. ___ PRIVATE PURCHASE 03. ___ MILITARY 04. ___ OTHER:

E15   To the nearest thousand dollars, how much did you earn last year in net after paying truck expenses, including any interest on loans on the truck(s)?

    ☐ DOLLARS

F. TECHNOLOGY

F1   Now I am going to ask you some questions about the technology you use in your work as a truck driver. Which kind of 2-way communication device do you use most often to communicate with your dispatcher?

a. _____ Pay phone
b. _____ Fax
c. _____ Beeper/Message Pager
d. _____ 2 way radio (not CB)
e. _____ Cellular phone
f. _____ Personal Computer
g. _____ Automatic Vehicle Location
h. _____ Satellite Based system
i. _____ Mobile Fax

G. DEMOGRAPHICS

G1   RECORD GENDER BY OBSERVATION:

1. MALE	2. FEMALE

G2   How old are you?

YEARS OLD

G3   Are you currently married, widowed, divorced, separated or have you never been married?

1. MARRIED	2. WIDOWED	3. DIVORCED	4. SEPARATED	5. NEVER MARRIED

G4   How many financially dependent children do you have?

DEPENDENT CHILDREN

G5   About what was your total family income last year?

$_____   GO TO G6

PROBE IF NECESSARY:

G5a   Was it more or less than $30,000.00?

1. MORE	2. LESS

GO TO G5c

G5b   Was it more than $45,000.00?

1. YES	5. NO
GO TO G6	GO TO G6

G5c   Was it less than $20,000.00?

1. YES	5. NO

G6   Are you a military veteran?

1. YES	5. NO

G7   Do you consider yourself white, African American, Asian-American, Native American, or something else?

1. WHITE	2. AFRICAN AMERICAN	3. ASIAN-AMERICAN

4. NATIVE AMERICAN	5. OTHER

G8   Do you consider yourself to be Hispanic?

1. YES	5. NO

G9   What is the highest grade of school or year of college that you completed?
PROMPT IF NECESSARY ; RECORD CONTINUOUS NUMBER IF GIVEN.

01. LESS THAN HIGH SCHOOL (8th GRADE OR LESS)	04. VOCATIONAL OR TECHNICAL SCHOOL	07. COLLEGE OR GRADUATE DEGREE
02. SOME HIGH SCHOOL (9th - 12th GRADE)	05. SOME COLLEGE (NO DEGREE)	
03. HIGH SCHOOL DEGREE	06. ASSOCIATE DEGREE	GRADE/YEAR

G10   Did you ever take formal training to become a truck driver?

1. YES	5. NO

G11   Do you currently belong to a union?

1. YES	5. NO

Those are all the questions we have. Thank you for your time.

TIME NOW:

Notes

Overview of the Driver Survey

1. When the first day at a truck stop was a Friday, interviewers returned on the following Monday to complete their schedule.

Chapter 1. Who Was Interviewed

1. Although we asked drivers to identify the community in which they lived, concerns with maintaining anonymity precludes releasing this data.
2. One individual did not respond to the union membership question.
3. A technical description of the multistage sample design utilized in this study can be found in appendix 1.
4. These sum to more than 25.5% due to rounding.
5. Only a subgroup of the respondents in for hire were asked whether they worked for TL or LTL firms.
6. This might also be explained by the small number of owner-operators who have pension or deferred compensation plans (see figure 13).
7. The Outgoing Rotation File (ORG) of the U.S. BLS is the compilation of the data from the Current Population Survey (CPS) for the month in which individuals are asked economic questions. The CPS is a monthly survey that provides the national labor force information used for purposes such as estimating the unemployment rate. The CPS is collected by the Bureau of the Census.

8. Because so few drivers are under 21, we have limited our national blue-collar sample to individuals 21 and older in these comparisons.

Chapter 2. Driving Distances and Earnings

1. The upper and lower 1% of the mileage distribution, those reporting less than 5,000 miles or more than 200,000 miles in 1996, were trimmed from the distribution. This excluded very short-term employees and those reporting unrealistically high mileage.

2. Few union employees are paid as a percentage of revenue, and these were excluded from the analysis for statistical accuracy.

3. It may be that nonunion employees and owner-operators who load or unload trucks but do not get specific payments for such activities are compensated through higher mileage rates. This is not immediately apparent in the data, but it is difficult to separate out the factors affecting mileage rates without use of regression.

4. Bonuses may also be paid in the form of nonmonetary benefits. One major carrier rewards drivers with good mileage records with hotel rooms in a Florida, and arranges deliveries to Florida to allow the driver and his or her family to take advantage of these rooms.

5. Dr. Michael Belzer suggested this comparison.

Chapter 3. Hours of Work, Hours of Rest

1. The FLSA limits drivers to working no more the 150% of the forty-hour week established by the act. Also in contrast with the balance of the act, in which employers are made responsible for adhering to the act, drivers and employers are held jointly responsible for violation of the limit on hours. The exemption from the minimum wage provisions of the FLSA was originally provided because of the strength of collective bargaining in the industry.

2. Individuals reporting zero hours and zero miles driven in the preceding twenty-four hours were excluded from the sample. Those reporting in excess of twenty-four hours of work in the last day were also excluded from the sample.

3. Local drivers may be union employees, nonunion employees, or owner-operators in the general sample.

4. Individuals reporting zero hours of nondriving time do not include any who had not worked in the last twenty-four hours, as these were removed from the sample for the purpose of calculating these statistics.

5. These categories include local drivers.

Chapter 4. Job Tenure and Stability

1. Owner-operators are excluded from this analysis, as they are self-employed, and questions about their firms make little sense in this context.

Chapter 6. The Utilization and Effects of New Technologies

1. Maximum trailer length and height are established by state and federal law.

2. There are exceptions. For example, firms may provide a guaranteed rapid delivery service and charge a premium because they send trucks out only partially loaded.

Chapter 7. Regulation and Pressures on the Job

1. Firms are required to collect and review the logbooks and cannot legally dispatch drivers in violation of their on-duty hours.

2. Local drivers work under very different conditions than over-the-road drivers with many fewer problems with unrealistic schedules.

References

Belzer, Michael H. *Collective Bargaining in the Trucking Industry: The Effects of Institutional and Economic Restructuring.* Ithaca, N.Y.: Cornell University Press, 1993.

Cochran, William G. *Sampling Techniques,* 3rd ed. John Wiley & Sons, New York, 1977.

Goodman, R., and L. Kish. "Controlled Selection—A technique in Probability Sampling." *Journal of the American Statistical Association* 45 (1950): 350–372.

Kish, Leslie. *Survey Sampling.* John Wiley & Sons, New York, 1965.

Heeringa, S. University of Michigan Library Study, 1984.

Mishel, Lawrence, Jared Bernstein, and John Schmitt. *The State of Working American, 1998–1999.* Ithaca, N.Y., Cornell University Press, 1999.